Surviving With Serenity

Daily Meditations for Incest Survivors

T. Thomas

Health Communications, Inc.
Deerfield Beach, Florida

Publisher: Health Communications, Inc.
            3201 S.W. 15th Street
            Deerfield Beach, Florida 33442

Surviving With Serenity is a daily meditation book written by an incest survivor for others who have survived the betrayal of incest. The meditations are written in the spirit of 12-Step recovery, originally developed by Alcoholics Anonymous (AA) and applied to survivors of sexual abuse in such fellowships as Incest Survivors Anonymous (ISA) and Survivors of Incest Anonymous (SIA).

These are the daily meditations of one incest survivor and are not meant to speak for any of the aforementioned fellowships. I offer them to you as springboards for your own reflections.

Please do not disqualify yourself from reading this book for fear that it might not really apply to you—that "incest" might be too strong a word for the betrayal of trust that you experienced. You are not alone. At least one in three girls and one in six boys have been forced into some form of sexual activity before the age of 18. And that does not even include the many more who have been victims of voyeuristic looks, overly suggestive or sexually degrading comments and not-so-innocent touch in the name of hygiene or affection.

I invite you to use this guide in whatever way is most helpful to you. Pick and choose meditations, jump around or go day by day. You will find herein many concerns that incest survivors have. The themes came from women and men who are healing from the devastation of incest. Are you struggling with a particular issue? Check the index. You may well find a reference to that theme. If it is not there, call another survivor or write your own meditation. Do whatever it takes to heal.

As the subtitle suggests, this is a meditation book, a daily spiritual guide with the focus on healing from the effects of incest. Spiritual recovery may seem very natural for those of us who feel a strong presence of God, Nature or other loving Higher Power. Yet many survivors struggle with trusting the spiritual side of life, not knowing why the God of our childhood did not protect us from being abused or remembering how our perpetrators loved to invoke God or religion to justify their crimes. A major focus of this guide is letting go of the self-made "gods" of those who abused us and finding a deeper caring Source of love and healing who will not betray us—whatever we choose to call that Source. I will use the term "Higher Power" because it is so common in 12-Step groups. Let your heart read it as your own Inner Guide directs.

A suggested prayer or affirmation is offered at the conclusion of each day's meditation. Hold it in your heart during the course of the day or otherwise use it as you find helpful. We have internalized so many negative abusive messages about who we are (and replay them over and over again) that we have forgotten how beautiful, precious and lovable we are. These meditations are about remembering how dear we really are and discovering the "God within."

Wherever you are in your process, know that you are a person of beauty, a person of courage, a person of strength. You deserve the healing and new life you are now seeking—and so do I. We cannot rewrite the history of our victimization nor bury it any longer. But we can receive the gift of healing which is offered us one day at a time in this new way of surviving with serenity.

In Healing Love,
T. Thomas

Beginnings and endings can be both far apart (as in January 1 and December 31) and side-by-side (as in December 31 and January 1). The latter way of looking at this is probably a more helpful guide for living as incest survivors. This way we can live life as it comes, rather than by mulling over a distant past or planning far ahead into the future.

Living one day at a time is a process of continual discovery and renewal. Sure, difficulties can arise — but we only have to deal with them for today. Daily beginnings and endings lead to a continuing interplay of openness and closure.

God, grant me no more than I can handle this day, and tomorrow let me begin anew to discover life.

Recovery from sexual abuse is a continuing process. The first stage of that process is recognizing that we were victimized — often by a person we had trusted. This may well be the most difficult step of all because it means that something was inflicted upon us over which we had no control.

It is scary to feel powerless. For if when we were powerless we were sexually abused, could not acknowledging such powerlessness open us to further abuse? Pretending the abuse never happened or that we were to blame for it can put us in more danger of being revictimized. We cannot protect ourselves from what we pretend is not there. Admitting we were abused is our first step to freedom from the victim-perpetrator-rescuer triangle.

Help me to let go of victimization by first feeling all the feelings it has brought me.

If you have been sexually abused at any time in your life and are now reading this meditation, you are a survivor. Being a survivor does not mean we are no longer victimized in any way. Some of us are still being sexually or emotionally abused. Many of us continue to victimize ourselves or to find ourselves in situations in which we are revictimized. Yet we have somehow survived the initial betrayal and trauma of abuse and are now searching out a way of healing. And for this we are to be congratulated.

The difference between being a victim and a survivor is that survivors have hope of a way out of the devastation of incest — a realistic hope. We find and network with other survivors, sharing and striving for new life.

I have survived!

From victim to survivor to thriver is the life-giving path we follow.

As victims we knew oppression rather than freedom. As survivors we did what we had to do in order to keep on living and functioning against great odds — but we were still burdened by the effects of our victimization. As thrivers we grow and flourish, living life as we were meant to do.

Thriving does not mean we forget about the abusive past nor that we never feel sadness, for the scars of incest always remain. But as thrivers we are free to live and to love. Because we have deeply felt life's suffering we are all the more open to experience life's blessings as well. We no longer merely exist or survive, we thrive on life.

Higher Power, plant me where I may thrive.

Serenity is a way of living that is a gift of our recovery. It includes an ability to accept ourselves as we are, live life at its own speed and trust the guidance of a Higher Power on a daily basis. Serenity is a quiet assurance of the okayness of our being in life.

Serenity is a long way from trauma and is its perfect antidote. However, serenity is neither denial of trauma nor numbness to it. It involves an ability to deal maturely with whatever happens without sacrificing our integrity.

Serenity is the antithesis to a life of turmoil. It is a very attainable goal for those who have been victimized by sexual abuse. It is no longer sufficient for us just to survive; we need to survive with serenity.

May I survive with serenity.

It is not uncommon for we survivors of child-hood sexual abuse to grow into adulthood hating ourselves. We may not know why, but such behaviors as attempted suicide, eating disorders, drug and alcohol abuse, perfectionism, sexual addiction and workaholism — whatever else they may indicate — carry a large dose of self-hatred.

Self-hatred, self-blame and low self-esteem walk arm-in-arm down the streets of our lives. Whenever something goes wrong, we feel it is our fault.

Healing from self-hatred requires the willingness to admit personal powerlessness over others, especially those who abused us. This can be a very scary step but we need not take it alone.

I choose to acknowledge the painful reality of my having been abused rather than clinging to fantasy and self-hatred.

6

In recovering from the devastation of incest, many of us are only beginning to view our family of origin in a clearer light. The abusive aspects of our family we have either reasoned away or blamed ourselves for.

The healing process for each of us is related but different. Some of us were abused by a parent or parents, others by siblings, still others by various relations or family acquaintances. We might be ready to recognize and confront the abuse and the abuser, but other family members might still cling tenaciously to denial and become angry at us for raising the issue. Whatever our choices, it is for ourselves alone that we are responsible.

———————

My family of origin brought me into life. Now, as an adult, I alone am responsible for how I choose to live it out.

We cannot live unless we breathe. And yet so many of us forget to breathe. Oh yes, we draw enough air into our lungs to survive but not to dissipate and let go of the constricting fear. How often do we find ourselves heaving an involuntary sigh? That is because we have just taken air into our lungs after a period of constricted breathing.

There are many cues that can trigger our old fears. We react as we once did when we were about to be abused. We freeze up. We become paralyzed and unable to breathe freely. For some, it might escalate into a panic attack with hyper-ventilation as well.

Part of the healing process is reclaiming our breathing. It is our right to breathe deeply of life.

Breathe!

Healthy parenting is an experience most of us did not have. We came from dysfunctional family systems. Often because of our parents' emotional immaturity, we as children assumed a parenting role.

As adults we have the inner child of our past still very much alive inside ourselves wherever we may be. Healthy parenting begins by learning how to listen and respond to the needs and feelings of our inner child.

We do not have to be the perfect parent to our inner child or our natural children. All that is required is a willingness to be loving, open, vulnerable, nurturing and protecting. Healthy parenting has a great reward: the opportunity to see the child flourish in an atmosphere of love.

Help me to become an accepting and loving parent to my inner child.

Surrender — what a frightening word, inviting flashbacks and feelings of helplessness and submission to a perpetrator! And this same word is supposed to be a key to healing and recovery? Yes. But there is a big difference between surrendering to inevitable abuse and surrendering to the Source of healing, guidance and love.

In recovery there are two major differences for us. First, our healing surrender is a personal choice, not something forced on us as was the abuse. Second, the Source of our healing (God, Higher Power, etc.) always offers guidance out of love.

When we surrender to that Presence which is deep within us, we are saying no to the pretense that we can do everything on our own. Surrendering means laying down our weapons and becoming vulnerable to our Higher Power.

Help me learn to surrender to Guiding Love and not abuse.

Incest survivors can go through life wearing some very heavy armor. Some of us have tried to put layers of clothing or body fat between ourselves and the world. Whatever protective measures we have taken, there is always a scared child on the alert (hypervigilant).

We may or may not feel as though our guard is always up. But our bodies tell us. Is our breathing constricted? Do we have rock hard shoulder, neck or other muscles due to constant tension? Is a queasy stomach our constant companion? Do we suffer from high blood pressure or migraine headaches? Repressed feelings and hypervigilance can lead to any or all of these conditions.

Healing recovery, conversely, leads us to recognize that there is a Higher Power who loves and guides us unconditionally.

Guide, protect and defend me from harm. Grant me the openness of a child to the beauty of life.

Readiness is the healing counterpart of hyper-vigilance. For those of us who practice the 12 Steps, readiness involves a time of action and one of active patience. The action comes through a personal housecleaning that includes letting go of self-destructive behaviors and learn-ing to love ourselves and others in a healthy way. The active patience is needed for trusting our Higher Power to take the active lead in removing our self-destructive behaviors and of-fering us lifegiving guidance.

In hypervigilance we rely totally on ourselves but with readiness we make space — so that our Higher Power can supply the grace of growth. Yet none of us has to choose this path unless/until we are ready to do so.

I am ready for the next step of healing and growth that will be offered me through grace.

Healing from incest is a process that can take many years. Often a person may be between 20 and 70 or even older before remembering the childhood sexual abuse. Along with the flash-backs can come a deep regret that we have spent so many years of our life in unknown fears and self-destructive behavior. How do we deal with these feelings and recover from incest?

It is important to remember that our amnesia or repression of incest memories helped us to survive the trauma of abuse. We forgot because it was too painful to remember. Now that we remember, it is not less painful, but we are better able to bear the pain and to seek out resources that will help us heal and live healthier lives.

I am at the perfect age for healing and learning to live more freely.

Frozen rain brings the world to a standstill. Cars spin like tops on newly glazed roadways. Pedestrians struggle to keep their balance.

Even the fearless respect Nature's icing of the earth. "Don't go out!" is the sound advice given. Yet the icing often happens quickly and without warning. The best we can do is wait for the sander or a weather change. We have to recognize our powerlessness, let go and let God.

Flashbacks are often the ice storms that hit survivors with very little warning. It is important to recognize our powerlessness, let go of whatever else we are trying to do and let God provide us with the means for getting back onto our feet with "traction" once again.

Be my safety on the slippery ground of flashbacks.

Exercise is a wonderful way to get in touch with our bodies and the life force within us. Many of us separated from our bodies during the times when we were abused and we still have a tendency to "space out" when we feel threatened or anxious. Exercise helps us to live in our bodies once more.

A simple exercise like walking helps us to breathe more deeply and regularly, thus releasing tension. We use and feel our muscles, recognizing them as part of us, rather than a separated "it." And we are drawn to take notice of our surroundings, the world of which we are a vital part.

At one time we could not run away from abuse nor overpower our abusers, but now we are truly *exercising* our freedom.

I choose to exercise my right to physical health.

There are different expressions for the feeling we have that something bad is about to happen: apprehension, impending doom, anxiety, panic and so forth. Our senses become hyper-alert. We start to feel paranoid. Our mind focuses on something terrible. Muscles tense. Maybe a headache comes.

A dark cloud has settled over us and we are gripped by a fear of the unknown. Oh, we might give that fear a focus, such as our car is about to break down. But the fear is much more basic than that.

We were betrayed. Our childhood trust was violated. Will it happen again? In our healing process we learn that the way out from under the dark cloud is in learning to trust ourselves and the care of a Higher Power who guides us.

Grant me the courage to risk trusting You.

Centering is the effortless effort of remaining serene and at one with ourself, no matter what is happening around us. It is an effortless effort because it is a state within ourself that we open to discover rather than work to achieve. Centered behavior is foreign to dysfunctional families such as the ones in which we grew up.

There are different techniques that can help us learn how to center. Relaxing our bodies and focusing on our breathing is one. Various forms of meditation show us others. All involve the paradox of our becoming empowered by means of self-acceptance and letting go. Centering is an opening to the mystery of our selfhood, trusting in our innate goodness.

Higher Power, you are the strength I find at my center.

If there is anything more difficult for survivors to deal with than failure, it is success. We can live in fear and anxiety in anticipation of failures to come, but it is success which often puts us into a real panic. Longing for or daydreaming about success is not the same as actually achieving it. That is when the scary part comes.

Success means change. And change is frightening. Success challenges us to believe something good about ourselves, contrary to our feelings of self-hate and worthlessness. True success is a combination of our own efforts and the grace of a Higher Power — and it is frightening to acknowledge our need for help or to risk trust.

May I receive success in a spirit of gentleness, humility and self-respect.

Incest survivors are vulnerable to getting caught in abusive relationships. Unfortunately we often end up being drawn to someone very much like our original abuser. We may expend a great amount of energy trying to "save" them or change them into the loving parent we never had. In fact, what is far more likely is for this person to abuse us in ways reminiscent of our primary abuser.

We need to abstain from abusive relationships as an alcoholic needs to abstain from alcohol. We need to feel the pain of our primary betrayal in a supportive atmosphere so that we can appropriately rage and grieve our losses. Only thus having gained a clearer perspective on our own life can we begin to seek out loving and healing relationships with others.

I deserve love, not abuse in relationships.

Growing up the way we did, we really do not know what normal behavior is. We may have ideas of love, care and nurturance, but they are often separate from our firsthand childhood experience. So we become hypervigilant observers in a world in which we think almost everyone knows the secret to normality but us.

In fact, we did not grow to adulthood without having at least one special person love and care for us. As we begin to feel our pain and to heal, we may be able to accept love from a dear friend who offers us what mother or father was not able to. If we try to *make* such persons "mother" or "father," we will lose an adult relationship and may alienate them altogether. But we can look to them as real life models of healthy love.

Help me to learn from lifegiving models.

In looking to others for guidance remember we also have valuable inner resources that can be tapped. It takes a lot of resourcefulness to survive childhood sexual abuse — and this is exactly what we have done. We can now learn to use our resources for our new way of life as survivors.

How do we learn? A spiritual advisor or sponsor — someone who has walked the healing path before us — can help us tap into our unique gifts. Prayer and meditation also can open us up to inner guidance. We are not alone. We are guided by a loving Higher Power.

Thank You for the inner resources that lead to renewed life.

21

We are not unlike the earth which has been raped and polluted by those who will not respect it. They raped Nature's beauty because they thought they had power, thought they had the right, thought that Nature would not stop them or cry out. They did the same with us. We are Nature too.

We wondered where God was in all this — for so many of us were raised to believe in God. Our abusers would have had us believe that God condoned the abuse because we were "bad." That was an outright lie. Was not God instead in the mountain lake raped by acid rain and in the little child raped by a parent? Was not God raped too?

I am of Nature; I am of God.

When we grow up with a world view that no one is to be trusted and that we are terrible persons, how can life be colored except in fear and suspicion?

Our abusers themselves lived in a frightful world. This was the sad inheritance they passed on to us.

It is true that we cannot prevent nightmares or those sudden fits of anxiety. But we can choose to deal with them instead of allowing them to color our world black. We can say the Serenity Prayer, call a sponsor and share our feelings, affirm the goodness and value of ourself and turn over the fear to our Higher Power. If we do what it takes to remain honest, open and willing to grow, we will not fail.

Every day I choose to let go of a little more negativity so that I may trust the goodness of life.

There are 12 suggested steps, 12 traditions and a few slogans in healing fellowships for incest survivors which base themselves on the spirituality so successfully developed by Alcoholics Anonymous (AA). "Keep it simple" is an important continuing reminder that our healing process needs to remain uncomplicated and uncluttered. Consciously living "one day at a time" while placing our trust in the care of a loving Higher Power provides the basis of our simple roadmap.

Keeping it simple involves asking God into our center every morning and every night in order to place "first things first." In so doing we are placing our trust more fully in the care of our Higher Power. We become open to grow as we use the simple basic tools offered us in our incest survivor fellowship.

Keep it simple.

Sometimes it seems life would be so much easier if it were all black or white, right or wrong, good or bad. As children we needed our parents to be all good, caring, strong and protective. They were not. So we continued to paint them in white and color ourselves in black — believing that the pain, shame and humiliation we felt must be all our fault.

As adults trying to survive, we might have continued this color scheme, by being quick to forgive or reversing it by seeing ourselves as innocent victims and them as evil perpetrators. This is a necessary step to healing but our world would still be black and white.

When we have exhausted our taste for black and white, we may open our eyes to realize there are a multitude of other colors with which to color our life.

Help me find color in my world.

Ambivalence in our feelings towards persons, places and things is the price we pay for risking to bring color into our world.

Having allowed ourselves our spectrum of feelings, now what? How do we deal with our feelings of hatred and betrayal for what a parent might have done to us if we also feel genuine love for that person?

There are no easy answers in the realm of ambivalence — we have conflicting feelings toward a person. If we consider the person important enough to us, we may want to work with our ambivalence. If not, we may want to withdraw. If we choose to relate, then we set boundaries; we make adult decisions for our well-being. And if things do not work out, we have the right to change our minds.

I have the right to make choices; I also reserve the right to change my mind.

One of the most damaging aspects of the incest experience is that our perceptions and feelings were not validated by others, and if accepted at all, they were likely distorted.

Validation often comes about when we share what happened to us and others respond with acceptance. One of the reasons that survivor meetings are such a powerful healing force is that we are there with others who share similar experiences of incest and betrayal.

Validation of what happened to us can begin by hearing other survivors share their stories. Initially we may feel for them what we are not yet able to feel for ourselves. Through such contact, the process of validating our past experiences has begun.

I did not imagine the abuse that was perpetrated against me.

We are not used to putting first things first. We are used to putting others' needs first and having distorted notions of our own. Many of us learned from our earliest days to take care of others and neglect ourselves. Such a lifestyle breeds resentment, whether we are conscious of it or not.

As we do not know how to care for ourselves, we often end up with overindulgence instead of nurturance. Some have become addicted to alcohol, sugar, illegal or prescription drugs, status, spending or promiscuity. We long for love and satisfaction but have no idea how to achieve it.

12-Step recovery programs help us find what we long for by teaching us to put first things first, which means letting go of self-destructive behavior, as well as learning to care for ourselves instead of trying to manage the lives of others.

First things first.

Healing spirituality is not the same as religion. It is more basic than that and more profound. To be open to the spiritual life means to be open to relationship with a Higher Power or Deeper Reality which is not identical with ourself. Ironically, the more open we are to a relationship with a Higher Power, the more open we become to a fuller relationship with ourself and with others.

Incest survivors, whether we call ourselves believers, agnostics or atheists, are all spiritual people. Abusers often invoke religion and God to justify their actions, when in actuality they live in isolation, cut off from a real sense of spirituality. Recovery is a spiritual process based on a healing relationship of trust in a Higher Power.

My healing spirituality is stronger than the chains of incest.

We who are healing from incest have under-
taken a journey from victimization to surviving
to thriving as human beings. The abuse was so
destructive because it isolated us. The only "support" available in such a place was that which
reinforced our silence, "badness" and the abuse
itself.

And so our movement from isolation to liberation involves making supportive healing connections.

It is a sign of strength to admit our human
limitations and to seek healing supportive relationships. We find our support in myriad ways
and places — in our Higher Power, through our
12-Step fellowship, in nature, in gatherings with
other survivors, in daily phone conversations
with our program sponsor, in a relationship
with a caring therapist and in trusting healing
friendships.

----

*I have the strength to admit my need for heal-
ing support.*

Perhaps the most painful reconciliation we will have to make during our healing process is between our mental consciousness and our body.

In order to survive, many of us viewed our bodily self as an "it," a "not me." And yet it was our body that bore the brunt of the attack. Loving ourself as an embodied person takes a lot of courage because it means coming back "home" into the physical self we once left because we were so vulnerable there. But this journey is necessary if we are ever to believe fully that the crime of incest was not our fault and that we deserve to reclaim our physical self.

Since loving our body can seem so risky, even overwhelming, we may find it best to begin a little at a time. Perhaps the most we can love today is a toe, a fingernail or an elbow.

Grant me the grace of loving my body.

Sometimes it is hard to say which are worse —
sleepless nights, those filled with unremembered
dreams or nights broken up by reliving the past.

The nights which disturb us so much are
actually a part of our self-healing process, leading
us through the feelings and memories to let
them go. Fear and anxiety often keep us awake,
afraid to let go into sleep when many of us were
formerly attacked.

Sometimes we have terrifying nightmares. Sharing them later with a trusted friend or therapist
facilitates our healing. They only have to listen
and love us — not even "interpret" our dreams
— for healing to take place. Other mornings we
may wake up exhausted, feeling we worked hard
all night in dreams we no longer remember. We
need to trust the inner process. We will be okay.

I trust the healing process of the night.

It is not possible to see our shadow if our life is lived in total darkness.

Healing can be extremely painful to begin with because the sunlight hurts our eyes that had become accustomed to darkness. It means handing back the shadows (guilt) that really belong to our abusers and other family members, but which we had taken upon ourself. Healing is a stepping out into the light with our whole person and risking acceptance.

We are not groundhogs who need to bury ourselves from the light of day. Will seeing our shadow scare us? Perhaps. But the shadow we cast is actually much smaller than our fears. Perpetrators deny their shadow and try to make others carry it for them; victims see themselves as nothing but shadow. Survivors and thrivers see both of these extremes as distortions of reality.

I have a shadow, but I am not all shadow.

Many of us grew up in alcoholic homes. A person does not have to be under the influence of alcohol or drugs to commit incest, but it frequently is the case. How many of us, in fact, have excused the actions of our abusers, saying they were drunk and did not really know what they were doing? Perhaps that is easier to say than, "My father or mother (or whoever) sexually abused me." Period.

As devastating as such a childhood was to many of us, it did not end there. Many of us grew up to marry alcoholic and abusive spouses. Many of us abused alcohol ourselves to numb our feelings. Some of us did both.

We need help. AA, Al-Anon or 12-Step fellowships for incest survivors can help us face the devastation of incest once we are willing to put down the booze or deal with our own co-dependency.

God, grant me the courage to reach out for the help I need.

We need one another. Incest was an experience that resulted in feelings of shame, humiliation and isolation. It was the ultimate in rejection and disempowerment. We need to come together with other survivors in order to discover that we are lovable, deeply wounded, but not alone.

Incest survivor gatherings of various types offer us an opportunity for validation, acceptance and empowerment. They provide a safe environment in which we can publicly share our feelings about what happened to us. They offer us hope, strength and en-courage-ment.

Gatherings offer us the opportunity to believe the truth of our own stories and feel our deepest feelings even as we listen to the feelings and stories of others.

We are healing. We are strong. We trust in a Higher Power of love.

Excitement can prevent us from getting in touch with our true feelings about the abuse. These can be scary and painful, but need to be accepted and processed. If our job involves "exciting crisis work" or we find ourself living in a crazy, unpredictable situation — it may well be time to assess ourself and our addiction to excitement.

Because we have numbed ourselves to the devastating aspects of the abuse, we may need lots of excitement just to stimulate ourselves at all — just to feel alive. But this type of stimulation is counter-productive because it is directly or indirectly self-destructive. The good news is that there is a happy alternative to excitement. It is called serenity and it comes about by living the steps of recovery in our lives.

_____

May healing serenity replace abusive excitement in my life.

36

Incest survivors are often known as super-responsible or irresponsible persons. But then our perpetrators did not assume their responsibilities to love us in a healthy manner when we were children. Nor did they take responsibility for the terrible crimes they committed against us. In response we might have developed an irresponsible helpless stance toward life or (and this is more often true) assumed responsibility for our abusers and every significant person in our lives.

We are only responsible for ourselves. This is true for every adult who has the mental capacity for self-care. Perpetrators assume no responsibility for their destructive actions. Survivors need to learn responsibility for self and find true empowerment by trusting in the care of a loving Higher Power.

It wasn't my fault.

For those who have had memory gaps or complete amnesia around the incest, the process of remembering can present a double bind. On the one hand we want to remember what really happened to us and why we have been going through life fearful and self-destructive. Yet remembering brings another kind of suffering to the fore.

Remembering may involve having memories without feelings but reconnecting with our feelings is essential in the healing process. Letting go of the awesome burden of abuse happens gradually when we can make these connections with a deep sense of love and compassion for ourself.

We need to trust our feelings. In doing so we become that healing child of loving Nature.

I remember that I am a beautiful child of a loving God.

Darkness can bring so many fears with it because we are unable to see. We have built our lifestyle upon hypervigilance. Darkness cuts back on our self-protective abilities by taking away our sight.

Darkness may put us in touch with the fear that the abuser would come. It feels as though darkness is the friend of the perpetrator.

As survivors we need to reclaim the darkness from our perpetrators. We need to assure our inner child that we will provide safety. As we befriend the dark corners of our souls, we can grow to feel okay in the outer darkness as well.

Darkness gives birth to dawn.

A spiritual way of life enables us to discover healing solitude where formerly there was destructive isolation.

Quiet times become sacred spaces that we treasure as part of our daily nourishment. Some get up early to read, to meditate, to center ourselves for the day. Others find a quiet time for reflection in a daily walk or swim or in time spent driving alone. The "daily double" of getting down on our knees every morning and night can be another form of connecting in quiet with the God of our understanding.

Through these we learn that solitude is far different from aloneness. We need not feel lonely in our solitude, but deeply connected at our center with all that is. Solitude is a precious means by which the 11th step bears fruit.

I can never be fully abandoned for You are always with me.

Gloom is the dark cloud that always seems to hang over us with the devastation that it threatens. Sound familiar? It should. It is the atmosphere in which we grew up, especially if our abuser lived with us.

We have grown up and our abuser is no longer a constant threat to us, but the feelings of gloom and doom remain. They can be triggered suddenly by almost anything.

We cannot prevent these feelings from arising in us. But we can respond to ourselves with love and care when they do. We can assure ourselves that we are in a safe place. We can break our isolation by calling another survivor or going to a meeting. If we do these things with a spirit of love for the child within, the feelings of gloom and doom will pass.

Higher Power, be a healing presence in me to withstand the feelings of gloom and doom.

Power may alternately attract and terrify us. We cringe at the thought of what power in the hands of an abuser did to us. Sometimes we scare ourselves with our own desire to use power in a vengeful way against those who wronged us. But violence begets violence. How can we become empowered and break the chain of violence at the same time?

The first step is to recognize that truly empowered people do not abuse children. Only the fearful, inferior and weak would choose to vent their violent passions against the innocent and vulnerable.

Healing is empowerment. Freedom to live our own lives is empowerment. Speaking out about the truth of abuse is empowerment. Becoming advocates for the innocent and vulnerable is empowerment. True empowerment fosters life rather than violates it.

God, grant me the power to live in love.

The 12 Steps of Alcoholics Anonymous have long been recognized as a deeply healing spiritual process for people suffering from a variety of afflictions in life. This is very true for us who have known the devastation of incest.

Today fellowships exist for survivors of sexual abuse that use the Steps adapted to their particular needs. These bear witness to the benefits of working the Steps through the healing and growth that can be seen among people in a program.

We will find no perfect people if we go to any of these meetings, for the Steps offer progress, not perfection. But we are likely to find people who are beginning to discover their lovableness and capacity to live more freely beyond the chains of incest.

The 12 Steps are my pathway from despair to new hope.

43

Once we begin going to step meetings we hear the phrase "the care of God" mentioned time and again as a vital part of Step 3. Yet most of us cannot help but question, "Where was 'God's care' when I was being raped and otherwise abused? Why should I trust now and risk more hurt?"

We cannot try to avoid dealing with this issue for long. Without beginning to trust in a caring Higher Power, we can have no firm hope of healing. We may then ask, "Have I allowed myself to hope only to be disappointed again?"

Coming to a fellowship for incest survivors we are beginning to trust in the care of a Higher Power instead of our isolated selves. It is "God as we understand God" in whom we trust, not the "God" of our abusers. We are letting go more and more of the image of a callous God cast in the image of our abuser and opening to the healing care of God.

Help me to trust in Your loving care.

"It works if you work it" is a slogan regularly heard at 12-Step meetings. There are two parts to this slogan which are equally important and empowering to incest survivors. By claiming both aspects for ourselves, we are transforming hope into reality.

"If you work it" implies that we have to take responsibility for our own individual lives. We are shown the steps and the tools of recovery; we are welcomed into a fellowship of persons who understand incest from personal experience. Now it is up to us to work our program of recovery. "It works" because finally the truth of our experience is validated. At last we are able to place our trust in a healing fellowship and in a Higher Power who genuinely cares for us.

It works — if you work it!

If we commit ourselves to a new spiritual way of living with the 12 Steps as our foundation, we can expect release from bondage to the past, happiness in the present and experience of serenity.

"The Promises," as they are called, can be found in *Alcoholics Anonymous*, more frequently called "The Big Book." But it is not only recovering alcoholics who have found these promises coming true; we incest survivors as well have found hope for healing from the devastation of incest and its after effects.

The 12 Steps work if we work them. Awareness replaces denial. Self-acceptance and a deep reverence for all creation replaces shame and self-hatred. Intimacy replaces isolation. And despair gives way to hope.

I trust in the promise of a new day.

Therapy can be a vital part of our healing process. In a counseling relationship it is crucial that we find a sensitive therapist. It is equally important that we leave a therapy situation that violates our boundaries or betrays our trust. The more we view therapy as a healing *tool,* the better we will be able to evaluate its usefulness to us.

It is with a caring therapist that many of us have first found acceptance and understanding, disclosing the incest experience. A non-abusive "authority" can be very healing as long as we do not make that person our ultimate Higher Power.

All persons, including the best of therapists, are limited and fallible; that is part of being human. Good therapy offers us a caring relationship which supports our inner integrity and helps clarify the truth of our experiences.

I need a helping hand in order to grow.

For those who have known the isolating effects of incest, survivor groups become an important basis for reintegrating our lives into all other types of groups, such as geographical, relational, religious, professional and social.

There are a variety of groups we may choose to enter with other incest suvivors. Some are therapist-led and some self-help, some are topical discussion groups and some 12-Step based, some are same-sex and some men-and-women groups. Each survivor must decide which type can be the most helpful at the present stage of healing.

Survivor groups offer a precious opportunity to break the hold of the abusers' lies on our lives. They counter isolation with connection, denial with acceptance, and disbelief with validation. They help us re-enter the various other groups in life that we find ourselves in — feeling normal, healthy and valuable as persons.

Survivor groups help me find strength and en-courage-ment.

Parents or guardians were responsible for raising the child we once were. Many betrayed or
violated us. But since the age of 18, when we
have been legally on our own, how have we
parented our inner child?

Have we, like our parents, been unable to
take responsibility for loving and nurturing, for
listening to, understanding and accepting the
child we once were and who continues to live
inside us?

We cannot change the damage done to the
child we once were. However, we can respond to
the inner child within each of us with love,
understanding and compassion. This takes a lot
of patience and listening at times, but it is worth
it if we love our child. Even if we are parents of
biological, adopted or foster children today, the
first child that needs our continuing love and
care is the child who lives inside ourself.

I love the child I once was — the child I still am.

Sometimes people who are angry clench their fists or teeth. The child "taken" by an older, stronger, more powerful person could neither escape nor fight, suffering fear and humiliation.

Years have gone by and we still clench. During the day our clenching can show itself in how we may hang onto money, people, possessions and opinions, or in the opposite — not be able to "catch hold" of anything.

We need to give the child within a safe and caring environment in which to relearn these processes of holding on and letting go without threat of betrayal and humiliation. By soaking in such supportive, sustaining, challenging love on a daily basis, we gradually give ourselves permission to let go of the need to stiffen and clench.

Help me gradually to open my hands and my heart to the gift of sustaining love.

Some of us have grown up to believe that we are no good because of the sex we were born with.

Such thinking comes from the fears inflicted on us by the abusers. This can keep us mistrusting and fearing one another so that we remain isolated from those who might offer caring support. It also locks us into denial. The truth is that neither all men nor all women are untrustworthy. The perpetrator alone is responsible for the destructive violence done to us. We alone are responsible for recovery.

Yet all alone we have little hope. Women and men survivors are coming together more and more to say that abuse is not a sex issue, but a *human* issue. And healing together as sister and brother is our newfound strength.

Our strength is in healing together.

For those who are survivors learning to listen to our bodies and to respond with compassion can be an excellent preventative medicine. We don't have to suffer so much if we learn how to take better care of ourselves.

As we begin to live the 12 Steps, we realize how out of balance our life has been. Our daily inventory, as part of Step 10, begins with how well we have taken care of our primary respon- sibility — ourself. And in those quiet moments of daily meditation we can feel the subtle mes- sages telling us that we might be "coming down with something."

By listening to our body in sickness and in health, we can learn to anticipate and care for our needs. We deserve it.

I deserve my own love and care in sickness and in health.

When is a person ready to deal with the damaging effects of incest? When is a person able to receive the healing that leads to new life?

Ancient wisdom tells us that when the student is ready, the teacher will appear. For us, memories and feelings will present themselves when we are ready to deal with them safely through the guidance of a Higher Power within that is wise and loving. Forcing the "forgotten past" to the surface prematurely by means of harsh or manipulative drugs or mind/body techniques — fighting Nature — causes more harm.

Whatever needs to come will come when we do not have to deal with this alone. Our Higher Power is the teacher who knows when each student is ready to embark on his or her healing journey.

Help me to say yes when the time is right for healing.

"I feel like a zero that cannot disappear."
"How long can I keep up this facade of keeping people from seeing that I'm nothing but a complete zero?"

It is okay to acknowledge that deep down we may often feel like a real zero. It was just one way that helped us to survive.

Often as children we could not afford to believe that our abusers were acting cruelly and unfairly. We took the blame on ourselves in order to make it through alive. Somehow we felt we were the zero the perpetrator hated. But something deep within us (our Center, our Self, our Higher Power) has always known that far from being a zero, each of us is a precious child who deserves love and nurturance.

I am God's precious child.

Incest was a destructive wall that blocked us from receiving acceptance. We might even have come to believe we did not deserve acceptance as worthwhile human beings.

But what happens when sensitive and caring people affirm our personhood? Can we afford to risk believing they may be right about us, that we have not just fooled them into seeing us as good when we are really bad?

This is not easy to do. Even though we deserve acceptance just for being human, *we* have to believe we do. Acceptance is a gift of our Creator who says, "I love the being I created." This gift is offered to us through others and can be found at the depths of our being.

Today I choose acceptance.

Nothing grows without sunshine. Nothing grows without rain. Life is neither all sunshine nor all rain. Both are needed for balance.

Do we tend to hide from the rain because it depresses us or live our life as though we were caught in a constant downpour? When was the last time we played in rain puddles or caught raindrops on our tongue? When was the last time we took a walk in the rain by ourself or with a dear friend?

We have experienced a lot of rainy days. But we do have a choice. We need to get away to a sunny climate for a while — that is, not to be obsessed with incest all the time. And maybe we need to learn how to play in the rain. Options and choices — sunshine and rain — are a liberating aspect of our healing process.

Higher Power, rain Your love on me.

Desire . . . longing . . . yearning . . . There are different words for the "unspeakable" at the depths of our being that draws us into relationship. Too often we have ended up in relationships which were destructive. Too often we have turned to substances or activities to try to fill our desire — but have never achieved success. Nonetheless, our desire will not leave us alone.

Ultimately desire is our longing to break out of the prison of victimization, our true self deep within longing for love.

Desire is stirred by that still small voice at the center of our heart that whispers, "You are beloved and precious." Desire grows from the image of the Divine embracing us in tender, unconditional love. Desire is the inner longing that will not be satisfied until we break the bonds of incest and find serenity in our true Home.

Higher Power, lead me to my heart's desire.

How can we possibly recover what we never had or that which was so brutally taken away from us?

There are some losses which can never be recouped — only grieved. We cannot go back to a loving, accepting womb that was not offered us in the first place. We cannot go back in time and change perpetration, co-abuse or denial into parental love and support. We cannot have the childhood family of our fantasy that would have loved and protected us.

But recovery is possible. We are recovering what our parents could never give us: a new sense of our true integrity, wholeness, lovableness, beauty, empowerment and grace. Yes, our losses are many. But they cannot compare to the new hope we are recovering day by day.

I am recovering.

Incest recovery can include times of unusual sleepiness. We may sleep later than usual in the morning and find it so hard to keep our eyes open on waking that we may go back to sleep. The same feeling may come over us again in the afternoon. And we find ourselves going to bed unusually early at night.

Asleep, we are filled with anxious dreams one after the other. The incest feelings are coming out of us, working through our bodies. We are beginning to let go. If we have a trusted friend or therapist, we may want to share our remembered dreams and feelings to help process them.

But basically we need to listen to our body and trust the process. This is a good time to elicit the support of fellow survivors. It is also a time to learn how to take care of ourself in a gentle, balanced way.

Whether awake or asleep, I trust in the caring love of my Higher Power.

Today is February 29. Three out of every four years it is missing from the calendar. It can be upsetting for someone born on the 29th to say: "According to the calendar I have no birthday this year or next year or the next year."

We incest survivors are like the people whose birthday falls on February 29. We know we suffered a terrible violation of self, but in many cases family witnesses just say, "Nothing happened." There is no corroborating evidence to validate our reality. There is a blank on the calendar of our lives.

Although we may never find validation from the perpetrator or colluding family members, we can find that missing piece within ourselves. And we find encouragement from other survivors who, like us, have family members who would rather pretend that nothing ever happened.

Help me to claim the reality of my truth.

"Night life" is often a contradiction for incest survivors. Some of us, terrified of the night ever since we were children, search in vain for a place we feel safe in. Others have become "night persons."

Night and day are part of a unified whole. But for us the two can become disjointed. The night can still hold monsters for the child within us. These are not imaginary monsters, but living memories of the betrayal we suffered.

The world sleeps at night, though not for perpetrators, and not for incest victims and survivors who must be on the alert. Our hope for recovery is that we can reclaim the night. We deserve to live in a world where night and day offer us safety rather than the constant threat of violence.

Grant me nights of safety and healing.

Keeping secrets and staying victims go together for incest survivors. The perpetrators manipulated us into silence about the abuse. And when the external abuse stopped, inside we continued to be abused by the heavy burden of secrecy.

Talking about incest is one major taboo we need to break for our own sanity and healing as well as for the sake of other potential victims. Breaking secrecy often happens in stages in the healing process.

First, we stop keeping the secret from ourself. In dreams, flashbacks or body memories we begin to realize the truth of what happened to us. We risk sharing it with a friend or therapist. Having received belief, acceptance and understanding, we begin to share with other survivors. With each stage we break the chains of victimization and claim our right to healing.

Secrecy about incest victimizes.

Two of the most deadly words that can be said to or by an incest survivor are: "Nothing happened."

Many of us learned to distrust our feelings and memories because we were not believed when we first tried to talk of the abuse or because it was too painful to believe that someone we needed could betray us so cruelly. Even after much validation and healing we can still have our moments of self-doubt: "Did it really happen or could I be making it up?"

We do not question ourselves or identify with the feelings of other survivors unless we are survivors too. Our migraine headaches, tears, sleepless nights, terrifying dreams, panic attacks or numbness of feelings have been our body's way of breaking through the chains of denial.

Denial is worse than a living death.

Often the unstated fear of incest survivors is that our needs will turn out to be so great we would be disappointed, frustrated and betrayed once again. So we do not ask.

Sometimes we float from relationship to relationship hoping one day to find one that will click. Yet no one can satisfy all our needs. But there is one person who can at least listen to them as they arise and decide how to respond to them.

Each of us is that person. Having needs is scary because we have to risk reaching out. Will we be betrayed again? Maybe. But now we can say no to abusive relationships. Now we can say yes to trustworthy people who offer non-invasive love and acceptance.

It is okay to say "I need."

We have ended up in isolation because the perpetrators denied their own isolation and tried to pass it onto us. Not anymore. We are taking charge of our lives by going beyond isolation. We are reaching out to other survivors and validating one another as sensitive, worthwhile, beautiful people who deserve more than a life lived in isolation.

Secrecy, victimization and isolation go hand-in-hand. So every time we go to a survivor meeting or share with another survivor the truth about what happened to us, we are striking a powerful blow against the isolation of incest. We are handing back the responsibility for isolation to the perpetrator and claiming another healing connection for ourself.

I am building healing connections by sharing and speaking out.

Incest results in death from the violence in-flicted by the perpetrator, by suicide later by the victim who cannot cope with a life of betrayal, or from dangerous substances or relationships the "former" incest victim is unable to escape. Un-checked, incest is a deadly crime that goes on killing its victims long after the physical perpe-tration has stopped.

But incest has not killed us who are reading this book. And we are determined to counteract its death-dealing blows to our bodies, emotions and spirits with hope for healing and a new life. Anyone who has physically escaped from the abuser can have access to this new hope. We are not alone. Together we can survive — and live. There is strength in incest survivors bonded to-gether by a power greater than ourselves. It is the power of Life itself.

As long as I am alive, I have hope.

None of us has ever been able to overcome the devastation of incest on our own. Why not? Because healing cannot be achieved in isolation. Healing requires a relationship with a Higher Power and other people.

As children we were powerless to prevent incest. As adults we are powerless to recover on our own. But in reaching out to healing fellow survivors we find a safe place that is both supportive and empowering.

The 12 Steps teach us that empowerment begins only when we first admit our powerlessness over the reality of the incest experience. However, we are not powerless to respond to it today. "We can" holds out the hope of healing in solidarity with other survivors.

We can.

When we stuff our feelings, we become the scornful disapproving parent who says, "Don't you dare say that! Don't you even feel that!"

When we stuff or deny our feelings, we do violence to ourself. And we may already be "paying" for such violence by suffering from migraine, hypertension, back aches and other bodily afflictions.

Stuffing feelings is a form of self-abuse. Just as our perpetrator had no right to abuse us, we do not have a right to abuse ourself — unless we insist it is okay to hurt or destroy that which is good and lovable. Each of us is that worthwhile person who deserves to be loved, not stuffed.

Higher Power, help me to deal with my "stuff" today.

There is also an underside to the trauma of incest called "loss." The betrayal of our personal integrity results in a loss of trust. And the traumatic relationship with the perpetrator often results in feelings of shame. Shame is perhaps the most devastating of losses because it is the loss of a sense of self-worth, goodness and value.

We who have been traumatized by incest can still have hope of healing. Why? Because the "true self" or core of "who I am" cannot be annihilated. Other personalities may arise to protect us in the meantime. But our true self is not gone, just in hiding — in the protective custody of other aspects of our personality. It is heard as the voice of our center saying, "I am with you always; I will not leave you." It is both our own voice and that of a loving Higher Power that will not let that which is precious (us) be lost.

I am rooted in hope.

Journaling makes our healing process more visible. All that is required is a willingness to sit down and write.

It is a very real way of getting a handle on thoughts and feelings we might not have been aware of. Somehow explosive feelings that confuse and control us on the inside become defused when seen on paper. In this light, journaling can be another tool in the healing process.

We can actually see our own process unfold as we look at journal entries made over weeks, months or years. We need such external reminders at times when feelings like "I have gotten nowhere" ambush us. At such times our journal becomes a written testament both to our progress and to our investment in the healing process.

I am writing for my life.

Body memories come in various forms. Tears, shudders, tremors, painful tensing of muscles, aching genitals, gastro-intestinal pains or cramping, headaches and vision problems are possible symptoms. Even when our mind is unable to remember the incest, our body does.

A certain touch or sensation can stimulate body memories. Our body is actually presenting us with a memory we need to process and let go. At such times it is important not to cause ourselves more pain by fighting to hold it back.

Sometimes visual or feeling memories will accompany body memories so that we are able to connect our bodily reaction with a past experience. If we are accepting and loving toward our body at these times, we will heal.

My body remembers what happened.

We incest survivors may prefer to be invisible. If we cannot be seen, we cannot be abused. But does not remaining invisible lead to neglect or isolation?

We have learned to avoid attracting attention so as not to be raped. Yet we are deeply wounded people in need of human love and affection. We cannot remain invisible and also hope to heal.

Being seen does not mean being a successful, public person that everyone knows. Becoming visible means sharing who we truly are with at least one other person. We are incest survivors and also people who are worthwhile. To risk being visible is to risk believing that "I matter."

Higher Power, I believe I matter to You.

Many incest survivors have been violated by psychotherapists, massage therapists and other "professionals" through manipulative touching.

Yet somewhere along the line many of us choose some sort of bodywork to assist in the healing process. The possibilities include Therapeutic Touch, Reiki healing, therapeutic massage, shiatsu, acupuncture, polarity, Rolfing, etc. Attempting some form of bodywork when we are ready to do so with a "safe" person (perhaps a recovering incest survivor/bodywork professional) can greatly aid our healing.

Therapeutic bodywork is something we can incorporate into our healing process as we see fit. We can thus experience non-invasive, healing touch within the boundaries we ourselves set. And we retain the right to say no at any time.

May Your loving touch heal my body.

The feelings of terror we incest survivors know permeate our body, emotions and spirit whenever we are catapulted back into the abuse. The terror may be in the form of a flashback or various present circumstances.

We can be terrified upon entering the city limits where we were assaulted or smelling the cologne the abuser used or walking alone in the darkness or being in an elevator with any person of a particular sex.

The terror will pass if we breathe deeply and regularly, entrust our present feelings to our Higher Power and assure our inner child that we will not allow any abuse to occur. Terror is a present reminder of our previous helplessness. Serenity is the reminder that while we are powerless over the incestuous past, we are not helpless in responding to the present.

Grant me serenity in the midst of terror.

Memories of the incest arise as we need to deal with them. Remembering is part of the healing process.

Not everyone must have specific memories of the incest in order to heal. But it is a process taking place in us — from dis-integration to re-membering. In other words, our life is becoming less a collection of dis-connected pieces and more a re-membered whole — a lifegiving unity.

We cannot re-member on our own; we need to rely on a power greater than ourself. After all, we were created by a Higher Power; so will our re-creation (re-membering, re-integration, heal-ing) come about under the loving guidance of that Higher Power. All we need do is accept ourself lovingly and trust the support of caring survivors. This includes loving acceptance of incest memories when and if they come.

Higher Power, heal and re-member me when-ever I am dis-integrated.

We survived the betrayal of trust (incest) without a sense of being involved in life, of having choices. This has often resulted in adult relationships in which we can be non-assertive, compliant and set up for further victimization.

Passivity leads to isolation because of imbalance in relationships. Any relationship that is not mutual is isolating. Moreover, an approach to life that sees no freedom of choice for ourselves is one in which we feel controlled and alone.

Passivity is a form of resignation. But rather than resigning ourself to life or abusive individuals, we can choose to *surrender* to the Source of life of which we are a vital part. We thus opt for inclusion over isolation, for active cooperation instead of resignation.

I choose to take action in my life.

As incest victims, authority was something we saw outside ourselves — in parents, perpetrators, God, society. As healing survivors we are beginning to find authority within ourselves.

During the healing process we learn that we can be the "authors" of our own choices. To ensure our use of authority in a lifegiving manner, we rely on the guidance of a Higher Power. In so doing we are reclaiming the power to live and to choose, which had been stolen from us.

As adults we need to trust our inner authority before any outside ourselves. From our own authority we parent the child within; from the authority of an informed and free will we make decisions for our life.

I trust in the authority of Your Presence within me.

Incest shatters every sense of reliability and control in our world. We may reclaim some semblance of control by pretending the abuse is our fault. Convinced that we are bad people, we may then set out to fool the world into thinking we are good by our perfectionism.

Unfortunately this childhood solution is doomed to failure. Our actual lack of perfection can further isolate us from others, before whom we feel utterly fake. Over time we remain perfectionists. The healing process helps break this destructive cycle by enabling us to realize that we no longer have to assume responsibility for the abuse. It wasn't our fault. We learn it is okay to be human, to make mistakes, to not be perfect.

I am a good, worthwhile, imperfect, growing human person.

Perceiving reality is difficult both for perpetrators and their victims. It challenges perpetrators to take responsibility for their crimes secretly committed.

At one time in our life we might have needed to believe that the perpetrator would never do anything to hurt us or that adults we might have dared to tell would never disbelieve us or ask us to forgive and forget. We were not strong enough to stand on our own and perceive reality.

There is such a strong taboo against "telling" that perceiving the reality of incest also becomes taboo. When the time is right, memories and feelings about the betrayal arise in us. We begin to perceive what really happened. And though we may still tend to deny our own perceptions, sharing them with others who are supportive can help validate the truth of our experience.

Help me to see and to understand the truth of my life.

The 12 Steps for incest survivors offer us a way from despair to hope. If we surrender to this simple program we will find healing — a way of surviving with serenity.

Coming to meetings, for instance, we find support, camaraderie and validation. But unless we are willing to go to any lengths to develop a new spiritual way of living — to live the Steps — we may never escape the imprisonment of incest. The Steps are our keys to freedom.

We need a sponsor to help us sort out the keys and to stand by us as we take the risk of trusting a Higher Power who is neither our perpetrator nor ourself. And we need to be reminded that we are people of courage and hope who will stumble but not fail as long as we are willing to follow this simple path one step at a time.

My healing is in the 12 Steps.

The healing journey is not for the faint of heart. We need to be willing to go to any lengths in order to heal. We may very well feel a lot worse before we feel better.

The only way out is through. We need to trust the experience of other survivors who have gone before us that our feelings need not destroy us or anyone else. We need not be revictimized. But we *can* be freed. We need to risk trust in a loving Higher Power and supportive incest survivors until we are able to love ourself.

The 12 Steps are a proven spiritual path of recovery. They provide the firm foundation that cannot be pulled out from under us no matter how rough life gets. This is important to remember in going to whatever lengths it takes to heal.

I am willing to go to any lengths to heal the wounds of incest.

One of the societal myths that has aided in the denial of incest is that child abusers are "monsters." Moreover, people might insist that a survivor who feels any love or fondness for the perpetrator could not have been violated.

It is easy to deny the abuse if the perpetrator could be very loving and caring at times and if others tell us that the perpetrator had a positive impact on their lives. While acting monstrously abusive in secret, incest initiators can also show a public face as a good father or a sweet grandmother.

It is more difficult to reconcile our own feelings of love and hate toward the abuser. Through all this we need to remember to love and care for ourself.

Help me to refrain from abusing myself or anyone else.

We incest survivors can be driven to do more and more with less and less satisfaction. We may not even give a second thought to all that we do or even ask why we are doing it.

We may try to outrun our own feelings and memories as if they were not a part of us! If all our energy is invested in "doing," it is hard to feel and remember. This harsh way of treating our bodies and spirits is another form of abuse.

Eventually our bodies rebel with exhaustion or illness. The human body has an inner wisdom which says, "I deserve care and respect." Our bodies want to present us with the memories and feelings of the past so we can stop abusing ourself and let them go. Hyperdrive is rebellion against ourself, against our own body. We deserve better than that.

Slow down and feel . . . and heal . . . and live.

Many incest survivors carry around a big club we use only to beat ourself. The urge to swing the club at our most vulnerable spot can catch us unaware. Then, all of a sudden, despite all our healing work, four little words pop into our head — "I made it up."

Why do these words, these thoughts, keep coming back to torment us when we thought we had come so far in the healing process? Why are we such doubters when our spirits, emotions and even our bodies still bear the scars of incest? Instead of trying to answer all the "whys," we might try something simple. The next time those words pop into our head, *don't swing the club!*

I didn't make it up. It happened. And it was terrible.

Just as the child in each of us needs love in order to live, our adult side needs a sense of meaning and purpose in life. Incest denies the possibility of unconditional love and a meaningful life. The 12-Step survivor program has shown us the way to a life in which we can find non-invasive love and a sense of purpose.

This new life is a gift we receive as a daily reprieve from the devastation of incest. No matter how badly we have been damaged, we believe that if we have survived to this point we can receive healing for our incest wounds. One day at a time we are discovering that we are lovable, worthwhile people and that under the guidance of a Higher Power our life has meaning and purpose.

By living the Steps and trusting in the guidance of our Higher Power, we receive a daily reprieve from hopelessness.

Today is a gift of love I choose to receive.

Sexual harassment is especially denied when it occurs within the home. Some parents think they have the right to make suggestive, lewd, teasing or aggressive remarks to their "own" children. Yet this is a violation of familial trust and respect.

Sexual harassment is a form of sexual violence. It can be more insidious than physical violence because the adult may never actually touch, but still invade, insult, degrade, embarrass and humiliate another human being. The child does not yet have the adult's rights to have a "no" and a "stop" respected.

We need to recognize our sexual harassment as cruel and abusive if we are to heal from its degrading and dehumanizing effects. We also need to affirm our right not to submit to further attacks.

Higher Power, help me to affirm the goodness of "me" which has so often been torn apart.

When we make a mistake, why do we feel rejection or reprisal is imminent?

Because we are survivors of childhood abuse. We were given very conditional love as children. We came to believe that the violence done to us was brought on by our own "badness," demonstrated by our innocent or inadvertent mistakes.

Does this mean we are hopeless? No. When we make mistakes, we need to assure ourself (especially our inner child) that we are still good and lovable. We can strive to demonstrate the reality of this belief to ourself by refusing to rehash old or current mistakes and by actively loving ourself no matter what.

It is okay for me to be human and to make mistakes.

Dictionaries define the experience of embarrassment in terms of felt self-consciousness. That is a very mild way of saying, "I wish I could disappear from the face of the earth."

Embarrassment is not foreign to survivors of childhood rape. Feelings deep within us say, "I am embarrassed to exist. I do not deserve to live. I am less than human."

Every time we respond with embarrassment, our blood pressure mounts, our stomach churns, muscles tighten and our face flushes. Our body is saying, "Something is very wrong." We need to reassure ourself that *we* are not wrong, but that sexual abuse is always wrong. We need not stay embarrassed by the cruelty of others who wrongfully assaulted us.

I deserve self-respect.

People have boundaries that deserve respect. We are people too. However, if there is never any mutual crossing of boundaries, intimacy is impossible and isolation results.

Any boundary crossing without permission can be received as an invasive attack not unlike childhood incest. Unconsciously we can be recipients or initiators of such "invasive action." Touching another person without permission, walking into another's space without knocking and being welcomed, holding or cuddling a baby indiscriminately and using sexually charged or aggressive language are but a few examples of invasiveness.

Can we truly respect another's privacy, integrity and need for personal boundaries if we do not know and respect our own?

Help me know, respect and appropriately safeguard my personal boundaries.

"Betrayed" is something which happened to us in the past. But we need not become permanently frozen there. We need not betray ourself in the present nor let the past control our entire life. Freedom begins with acceptance of the reality of what happened to us, acknowledgment that it was a violent crime against a vulnerable person and continuing validation of the feelings of our inner child.

Sexual violence strikes so deeply at the roots of human trust that its consequences can be felt lifelong. Our feelings about it, whenever they arise, are alive and important. Having been betrayed has a deadly finality to it; having feelings about it that change as we grow provides us with life-giving hope for healing relationships.

I refuse to betray the child within.

Incest survivors seem to go through life on "roller coaster" highs and lows.

Amusement parks wisely do not allow very young children to ride the roller coaster. But it is our inner child who usually experiences the roller coaster extremes of emotions — longing for "unreachable" love while fearing imminent doom. When caught in either (or both) we need to find some grounding in reality.

At those times when our child is feeling "high" or "devastated," we need to offer an assuring, understanding presence. When the child is calmer, some reality orientation might help. The convergence of our inner child's feelings with our adult understanding does help us feel more together and balanced. Back on an even keel, we are better able to avoid the roller coaster extremes.

I deserve to live on an even keel.

It is relatively easy (if terribly painful) to say, "I was abused because I was bad." Or: "Yes, it happened, but there were times of loving too."

All of these distortions mask a deeper fear in us — the fear of finding out we were unwanted, the fear that is realized in the awareness that we were childhood victims of sexual violence. It is natural for us to desire to be loved and cherished for our own sake. But what message do we receive when a trusted other makes us the object of sexual aggression rather than love?

That we were not wanted and cherished unconditionally is at the root of our deep pain. Acknowledging our feelings when we are ready allows us to open to the Source of Love that does want to love us with no strings attached.

Help me to realize that I am of God and am eternally loved.

There is within every incest survivor a Presence which somehow assured us as children, "I will never forsake you," when we felt forsaken by father, mother and "God." It has been our lifeline when we have felt adrift and our connecting link when we have felt isolated.

When the abuse squeezed all hope out of life, this Presence helped us find the smallest bit of self-worth to hang onto in order to survive. When we lost trust in a Higher Power, we found unconditional acceptance in this unnamed Presence.

We have had a Presence within that has preserved us from death and annihilation, that has enabled us to survive. The love of that Presence is more enduring than anything we have suffered. Herein is the Source of our continuing hope.

I hope in a never-failing Presence.

One in three children are victimized. Yet the occurrence of incest as a crime against children is not considered rampant. Why not?

The taboo of secrecy surrounding incest coupled with we victims often taking the blame on ourselves has left us unable to realize that sexual violation happens to one in three children — by conservative estimates. We are those one in three children who have grown into adulthood feeling alone, crazy, confused, guilty, victimized, betrayed, ashamed . . . As we reach out to claim our own healing and support, we are discovering the human tragedy of this crime being committed against one in three children. And we are discovering the human strength that comes from more and more of us "one in threes" joining together for mutual healing and advocacy.

I refuse to stand by idly while one in three children continues to be sexually victimized.

Healing from incest can be exhausting work. Two helpful perspectives to keep in mind are: (1) In time it will pass and we will feel freer, lighter, more energized; (2) Living in denial also sapped our energy.

When we are exhausted we need healing rest. "First things first" is a helpful slogan which reminds us that taking care of our health and well-being has priority over other concerns, projects or persons.

We are vulnerable when we are exhausted, so we may need to take some safety measures. We will want to make sure the place we choose to rest and sleep feels "safe" to us. It is also helpful to have the phone numbers of therapist, close friend and supportive survivors nearby to share our feelings *after* we are well rested.

I welcome healing rest.

It only takes one betrayal of trust by incest to turn our stable world topsy-turvy. We can feel caught in a world that offers little safety. We wonder if anyone or anything (including ourself) can ever be trusted again. Trying to control our world as best we can to prevent the recurrence of incest, any change can be threatening.

There is no way around it, however. Change happens in life. And it will happen once we commit ourselves to the healing process. This is very scary in the short term. But over the long haul it offers us hope that we need not be chained by our past experiences or fears. With support from others and the willingness to take one step at a time, we can risk facing the changes that healing brings.

I am willing to risk change for the sake of new life.

For incest survivors, criticism can feel like rejection, whether we are being criticized or initiating the criticism of another.

Criticism exposes vulnerability. Vulnerability means "the capacity to be wounded." Thus, the person who initiates criticism (even if it is ourself) can feel like a rejecting abuser. Because criticism is often voiced by someone who is also angry and because we have come to equate the expression of anger with abuse, criticism as abuse seems to us the more likely conclusion.

Yet criticism can truly be constructive, lifegiving, healing if shared in love, openness and vulnerability, not in anger or defensiveness. The more we believe in our inner worth and value, the less we need fear criticism.

I choose to use criticism as a healing light rather than as a stabbing knife.

97

Victims of incest are or were vulnerable persons.

Our society disempowers people under the age of 21 and over 60, all women and the mentally, physically or emotionally "less than perfect." We are often cast into a more vulnerable state because of our being in a "minority." Anyone in our society, not in a position of power and control, is vulnerable. And perpetrators take advantage of any vulnerability to commit the crime of sexual abuse. They did so with us and, given the opportunity, will do so again.

Yes, it hurts terribly to realize we were victims of oppression and could possibly be again. But recognizing the truth of what happened can be a gateway to safer, more responsible living. We can turn vulnerable victimization into empowered advocacy.

May I be an advocate for those who are disempowered by society.

We had a very serious crime committed against us. The effects of sexual abuse are deep and long-lasting.

Yes, sexual abuse of children is not something to make light of, nor is the healing process. Recovery can be very hard work. That is why we need to maintain perspective along with a sense of humor. This helps us make it through a situation we felt was so hopeless.

Balance is a great aid in recovery. We are serious about our healing process and advocacy for those who continue to be victimized. But we also appreciate the ability to laugh at ourself. A healthy sense of humor keeps us in touch with the earth (humus) and our own body — the space where we live. Humor based on self-acceptance helps us to be serious about our healing work.

May I find laughter as well as tears.

Each of us was the object of unhealthy desire that abused and destroyed under the pretext of love. This taught us to distrust the possibility that we could ever be a "beloved."

And yet deep within each of us is a small voice which whispers: "You are my beloved." It is both part of us and beyond us. Some call it God or Higher Power, True Self or Deeper Reality. It is our ultimate Source of unconditional love.

Recovery leads us beyond the lies of abusive desire to a discovery — that we have all along been the beloved of someone who will never betray us. In healing we are led to discover the basic message of the Inner Voice: "All I want you to know is that I love you."

I am loved.

We turned on our "alert" and "danger" buttons when we were living in situations where the threat of abuse was imminent. But those buttons have stayed stuck in the "on" position years after we moved away from the perpetrator. We have come to feel "abnormal" if we are not hyperalert. And the state of being worried, as uncomfortable as it is, has come to be associated with at least a modicum of protection against "imminent" rape.

If we learn how to love and care for ourself and how to ensure our self-protection to a reasonable degree, we need not worry all the time. *Worry does not protect us from sexual assault.* In fact, it can hinder clear thinking and action that is self-caring. We need to trust less in the worrisome inner critic and to risk trusting more in the inner Healing Source of a higher nature.

I want to risk letting go of constant worry.

A childhood violation of personal boundaries gave us little basis to judge our need for privacy as adults.

Often as children we were told we were "bad" if we did not allow our perpetrators free entry into our rooms, our personal effects, our very bodies. We were led to believe that our natural desire for modesty, privacy and personal integrity was prudish, or "unfairly withholding."

Each of us has the right to define our personal boundaries. It is helpful to test them out, not in isolation, but with the help of a caring therapist, close friends and trusted survivors. We cannot risk intimacy if we do not have a separate, private self that we may choose to risk in relationship with another.

It is okay for me to cherish my personal space.

Our feelings toward perpetrators of incest can run the gamut. At times we have felt intense hatred for the abusers and even harbored fantasies of revenge.

If our revenge would involve acts of violence, we would only trade being a victim for being an abuser. It is best to work out our rage physically and symbolically under the guidance of a trusted therapist, doing violence neither to ourself nor anyone else.

The best "revenge" is to work actively on our healing. We deal a severe blow to the perverted system of abuse by refusing to act either as victim or abuser. Instead, we wreak vengeance on death by choosing life. Our revenge is to transform victimization into survival and a thriving new life.

Recovery is the sweetest revenge.

Religion can be a valuable tool in healing for many of us. It gives us a particular framework to live out the principles of spiritual healing we are learning through the 12 Steps. Those of us who choose to be active in religion do so in order to experience ourselves as unconditionally loved by a Higher Power, to let go of unhealthy guilt and shame and to enhance the quality of life.

Yet religions can be perverted into abusive creeds to reinforce the victimization of the powerless and to demand inappropriate forms of forgiveness and tolerance. Such "religious" attitudes are counter to the healing process. True religion is known by its fruits of healing, love and serenity.

There are many paths to the Source; may I be guided toward a lifegiving one.

Arrogance says, "I can do it alone." Arrogance needs no "God," yet unknowingly worships many "gods." Arrogance looks bold and strong and abrasive. Arrogance is a nine-letter word for "fear."

Arrogance pretends to stand above all others because it fears it is below all. Arrogance says, "I need no one," for fear that no one will accept, receive, love. Arrogance is the loneliest boldness of all.

Arrogance is puffed up — only because it is hollow. Arrogance is pretentious — because it fears its whole life has been lived under false pretenses. Arrogance distances others — because it is too risky to say, "I need you." Arrogance is a "luxury" which incest survivors cannot afford. For us arrogance is no less than a living death.

"Life-size" is my best size.

One of the benefits of attending survivor meetings is that we empathize with other survivors. It can be a revelation about ourselves when we feel deeply for another incest survivor before feeling okay about owning similar feelings.

Since in the past our feelings were vulnerable, we cannot now expect ourselves to trust others readily with spontaneous expressions of the self. It is somewhat easier at first to cry at another's painful story or to feel enraged at the abuse others have been subjected to.

Yet empathy is based on identification. I cry for you because I identify with you. Empathy can be a safe and supportive means of reclaiming my feelings for myself.

Feeling for you helps me to feel for myself.

Others can be confused when we react strongly or withdraw suddenly at a show of affection on their part. However, it makes sense for us to react this way when the "gifts" of affection we received as children were coupled with sexual demands.

It takes some relearning to realize that "I like you" does not necessarily mean "I want to have sex with you" or "I want to hurt you." Our culture is partly to blame when it teaches sexual behavior as the primary means for communicating tender feelings.

As we learn to trust others in our healing fellowship, we begin to experience positive feelings like respect, admiration and affection. By setting clear boundaries we begin to share tender feelings in relationship without the accompanying sexual demands.

Affectionate feelings can be safe and non-abusive.

We are not crazy. We are not rare. We are not bizarre. We were victims of traumatic betrayal too much for one person to handle — so we "split," dissociated. Some call us multiples — but that one title covers a broad range of survivor experiences.

When we first discovered the secret of our selves, some of us felt ashamed or believed we must be crazy. We are not. We were creative little persons who did what we had to do in order to survive. Each of the persons we discover as part of "us" had a role to play in our survival.

Now in the healing process we realize we have a gift of self-awareness that many others do not possess. Through self-acceptance and selves-acceptance we are learning to speak our own name(s) in love.

I love you; I have called you by name.

Anonymity, contrary to secrecy, allows us to have a safe place to share our stories with the trust that our boundaries and integrity will be respected. It provides a safe ground for healing and fellowship to take root.

Anonymity allows us to focus our advocacy on healing those who have been victimized and isolated by sexual abuse. At the same time, it downplays undue attention on a particular survivor.

Anonymity provides a safeguard for survivors in 12-Step recovery. It allows us to break our silence in a place where each of us can choose to identify ourself as an incest survivor or tell our own story.

Anonymity is the spiritual basis for healing in a 12-Step survivor fellowship.

Anonymity and speaking out about the reality of incest are not in conflict with each other. Rather, the principle of anonymity helps us to focus our "speak-outs" on healing and hope while avoiding the pitfall of self-aggrandizement.

Speaking out is best taken on when it aids our personal healing and serves as a means to share with others what we have first received. We incest survivors need to be aware not to speak out in ways that lead to a caretaking of others and neglect of our personal needs. That is too reminiscent of the unhealthy ways in which many of us were raised.

Speaking out can be healing and liberating. Through it we are breaking the bonds of enforced silence and offering a message of hope to others in need.

The truth of recovery is empowering; abusive lies only destroy.

The worst sexual abuse can be minimized. And many of us needed to minimize in order to survive. It was just too much to contemplate that someone we needed so much could betray us so terribly. So we minimized. And that was okay.

But today it is not helpful to continue to minimize our flashbacks, upsetting feelings, physical problems, sleep disturbances and other effects of the incest. We survived our childhood by minimizing, but that only postponed our having to deal with the reality of the sexual abuse. During the storm of abuse we took a "rain check" on facing its devastation. Now with the sunnier weather of support and care we can slowly begin dealing with the effects of incest without minimizing them any longer.

It happened. It was terrible. I can heal.

A Sudden Loss In Perspective — a slip — can strike an incest survivor from out of the blue.

The perspective we lose (sometimes suddenly, sometimes subtly) is that we are good, worthwhile, lovable persons. We then tend to abuse ourselves through use of addictive substances or involvement in unhealthy behaviors or relationships.

A slip can confirm our human imperfection, but it need not derail us from our healing process. To realize we have had a slip is to regain a clearer perspective on our life. The Steps are our daily guides to a new, healthy perspective on living.

If I could never have accepted the possibility of my slipping, I would never have risked learning to walk.

While 12-Step incest survivor fellowships do not have a formal organizational structure, we do have a means for coming together and networking among survivors and groups in a certain geographical area. It is called intergroup. Intergroup is a valuable tool to break out of any possible "my group" clique syndrome, to find empowerment in networking and to carry the message of hope to others who suffer in isolation.

At intergroup meetings we get to listen to and share with survivors from other groups, cities and even states. We can plan cooperative projects burdensome for any one group to handle alone. We get to experience that we are many hands, voices and hearts joining together for healing and speaking out to stop the crime of incest.

Help us to find the strength together that we could not achieve alone.

We can abuse ourselves today by postponing until tomorrow healing action in our lives.

Procrastination runs counter to the 24-hour program because it promises that we will start living, healing, recovering tomorrow. As the program clearly tells us, all we really have is today because tomorrow never comes. Thus procrastination locks us, who still feel we are victims, into the victim/abused role without hope for parole.

Procrastination is a way of saying that we believe we are hopeless but are too scared to admit it. A sure-fire way of dealing with procrastination and its underlying fear is to bring it to Step 1. Thirty days back-to-back reading and sharing on the first Step will help us focus where we belong — today.

All I have is today.

We sexual abuse survivors need a safe place to let down our guard, relax and open to the vulnerable side of our self which needs healing. We need to feel that our boundaries are safe and respected.

It can be helpful to have a safe room for survivor meetings where we can go in privacy or with another when experiencing overload. An atmosphere of hope and support, not allowing behaviors or language which abuse ourself or others, needs to be fostered.

Openness and dialogue can help ensure that in meeting places there is a common, acceptable "safe ground" for being and sharing. Ultimately, there are no perfectly safe places except those we create within ourselves, in the company of trusted others and with the guidance of our Higher Power.

I am safe within myself.

Wholeness means completeness and integration of the varied aspects of ourself.

Admitting the reality of our betrayal and our inability to change the past is the beginning of wholeness. Pretending to others we are "altogether" blocks wholeness; accepting our disintegration makes integration possible.

Becoming whole is becoming real. It is learning to live in our body once again. It is learning to live with our multiples, if we have them. It is letting go of the fantasy family of origin. It is learning to live in a world which is not black and white, but a spectrum of color. It is realizing we will make mistakes — and sometimes have to make amends — that will ultimately enhance our personhood and the quality of our life. Though we are broken, we can become whole.

I pray that I may realize my wholeness.

Wherever the Post Office delivers mail can be a meeting place if we avail ourself of program pen pals.

Chances are, there is someone somewhere we can pen pal with who has a similar "different-ness." If our 12-Step World Service or Regional Intergroup cannot help us find an appropriate pen pal, there are plenty of survivor newsletters, information exchanges and other sources to ask.

A meeting by mail is still a meeting — it just takes longer. It is okay to have more than one pen pal, as well as not to be committed to a survivor pen pal for life. Those who have program meetings to attend can still pen pal with other survivors for recovery. It is a wonderful way to do service and find recovery.

Letters can be lifelines.

The first and most painful admission we will ever make in the healing process is identifying ourself by our first name and with the description "survivor of incest."

More admissions follow. We discover that we are not different from others who attend 12-Step survivor groups. Not only are we not excluded from the company of other survivors committed to healing, we learn not to exclude ourself from membership in the human race. We belong.

Admission to the healing process comes by the grace of our Higher Power, the support and validation of fellow survivors and our own inner desire to turn the doorknob and walk through. Our admission to recovery is closely connected with an honest desire to accept ourself as we are and to trust the healing resources available to us.

I admit the truth of my life in my wounds and in my healing.

We survivors of ritual abuse are incest survivors too. Some of us were abused by our natural family, others by a cultic "family."

We too belong within the healing community of incest survivors. The unspeakable acts so many of us endured and were made a part of — the violence, blood, excrement, dismemberment, mutilation, reversal of values, coercion to participate, along with the threats and psychic surgery to keep us quiet — were built on the common ground of all abuse: attempted murder of the human spirit, even though with us it was taken to the nth degree.

We are ritual abuse survivors supporting one another and finding a place of welcome within the community of incest survivors. We are breaking a deadly silence and finding new life.

We are finding welcome within a healing community.

Growth means change for the better, a movement toward health and wholeness. Although we desire healing and wholeness, the risk and change involved is very threatening to most incest survivors.

Rather than being overwhelmed at the prospect of growth, we need to remind ourself that growth comes primarily as an offering of grace which calls only for a response of willingness. Growth is a journey into new lifegiving frontiers both within and beyond us. It is not something we accomplish all at once, but one step at a time. And willingness is the first step.

Willingness opens the door to growth. Trust in a Higher Power empowers us to step through. And a network of supportive survivors encourages us to continue on the journey.

Grant me the grace to risk receiving your offer of healing growth.

Growing up in a dysfunctional family gave us little perspective on what reasonable happiness might be. We tend to overrate or underrate it, but do not see happiness as a normal part of life.

A preoccupation with incest (including denying its reality) robs us of the simple joys in living and an ordinary sense of happiness can become distorted.

We may need to remind ourself that it is okay to be happy without expecting abuse to follow. We may also need to discover that normal people do not define reasonable happiness as a constant state of euphoria. During our early healing work we may go through suffering temporarily. It gets better. A serene happiness is one which grows and deepens in us as we continue on our healing journey.

Self-acceptance is the root from which happiness sprouts, grows and flowers.

We are the new life springing out of the ancient motif of death and resurrection.

A definite change comes about in us who move through the process from victim to survivor to thriver. We move away from feeling as though we were the living dead into a place where life and love are able to take root deeply in us. We begin to flourish.

Once we lived in fear of both darkness and light — no escape from the threat of abuse. Now we become bearers of the light and energy of life. This change comes about through living a new spiritually-centered way of life. Abuse is not forgotten, but it is healed. In letting go of the victim role, we become advocates for our own well-being as well as for those who still suffer.

Higher Power, fill me with new life.

Every time we hear, *"You Are Not Alone,"* we are able to find a little more hope and comfort. It helps dispel the lies that isolate us — the lies of our abusers.

Shame, guilt and fear isolate us. The crime continues as long as we continue to be victimized by these self-destructive feelings. But we begin to find our way to freedom the instant we hear those healing words: "You are not alone."

We can contribute to breaking out of our isolation by discovering how we are not alone. Attending survivor meetings, reading recovery literature, phoning other survivors to share feelings and experiences, doing public speaking or writing on incest are methods of reinforcing our healing connections. We are a growing number coming together to share a message of hope.

I am not alone.

Light is an enemy of darkness (and of denial) because it exposes what was hidden.

Dysfunctional families are often closed and secretive. Sexual abuse is hushed up and never spoken of. The light of exposure is fearful and threatening to perpetrators and co-abusers alike. So they tell us that light is "sick" and that we are "crazy." Yet the light of truth is the only way to sanity.

Healing light hurts the eyes grown accustomed to darkness. But if we stick with it, we become "enlightened." We come to see clearly what the lies were and what the truth is. In our healing process we are moving out of darkness into light. Let us do so gently so as to give our eyes time to adjust.

Let Your light shine in my heart.

Why do some incest victims die at the hands of the perpetrators or take their own life while others live? Why are some locked up in mental institutions while others go on to achieve an externally successful life? Why do some grow up to perpetrate sexual abuse while others become kind and considerate adults?

Purely intellectual answers to these questions do not suffice. In the final analysis many have to say, "Somewhere along the way a caring God rescued me from a life of destruction and permanent denial."

To the next question — "Why me?" — we can only answer, "For our own healing and to carry the message of hope to others." What we have received is a gift (grace). Do we not say thank you and open the gift of love?

Thank You for the grace to live and love anew.

One of the results of our healing process will be a new sense of thankfulness.

Of course we are not thankful for the horrendous crime of incest. We become thankful to our Higher Power for leading us to discover a way of life in which we can find a sense of serenity, well-being and purpose.

As a result of incest we have often felt a deep inner emptiness. Some have tried to fill it with substances or behavior that ultimately are self-destructive. But through working the steps our emptiness is gradually replaced by thankfulness. It involves a growing awareness and appreciation of our being, our inner beauty and innocence, and our rightful place on this planet. Thankfulness is a spontaneous welling-up of the divine spirit within.

I am growing full of thanks for the gift of life I am reclaiming.

Many of us got caught in food, alcohol or drug addictions, compulsive sexual behavior or other self-destructive activity trying to numb the painful reality that we were abused and betrayed by someone we needed to trust and to love. We cannot heal from incest when our bodies are chemically dependent and our emotions are strung out.

If we are currently addicted, we need medically supervised detox plus a total commitment to a 12-Step fellowship.

When we start to become overwhelmed with feelings, it can be suicidal to try to self-medicate. Incest has had powerful, long-lasting effects in our life, and clear thinking and feeling are needed now. Clean, sober and abstinent, we face life in safety and with the support of fellow survivors.

I need to take life at its own speed.

If we are addicted to any chemical substance or obsessed with any person or activity, our minds and emotions are clouded and clear thinking is not an option we are able to choose.

When we are clean, sober and abstinent is the time to think and commit ourself day by day to a life of sober living. Such thinking needs to be renewed daily and often several times a day. Getting into the habit of sober thinking during times of serenity can help us through the rough times when we tend to lose perspective.

The slogan "Think!" is meant to help us refrain from impulsive reactions to situations. However, it is not a license to mull things over in our minds hundreds of times to feel safe and in control. "Think!" reminds us that with God's help we are ultimately responsible for our own life.

Think!

Prayer is any form of communication with our Higher Power, traditionally in terms of words, dance, music or ritual. Less traditional forms of prayer are gardening, poetry, art and communing with nature.

There are even more basic types of prayer for incest survivors. Heading the list is "liquid prayer," commonly known as crying. We may feel embarrassed, frightened and relieved by our tears. But what possibly could be a more powerful form of communication with our Higher Power than a non-destructive rage?

Tears of grief and rage are powerful prayers. When we are ready, we may find it healing to share this intimate side of ourself with a trusted person or our survivor group.

Thank You, God, for liquid prayer.

There is a tapestry of survivors that includes people of every race, sex, age, economic level, sexual orientation, religion or philosophy of life. Sometimes we may feel the need to bond together in small specialized groups for safety and trust and in order not to risk being vulnerable. Then this is where we need to start.

But if that is where we stop, we will never be able to weave our tapestry of healing or sew together our patches of "survivor quilt." Fear can keep us in our own little corners or safety groups.

We incest survivors become empowered together. We are speaking out for our lives, for our very survival and for the helpless who are still being victimized. Together we are weaving a tapestry in which each of us is a precious part.

Recovery happens together.

The warmth of the sun on a golden spring day, the warmth of the handclasp of a trusted friend, the warmth of a smile from one who loves us, the warmth of an inner feeling of security, serenity, and love — are some examples of our newfound intimacy with life. As we keep going to meetings and risking trusting others committed to this process, we find experiences of warmth becoming more frequent.

We discover that warmth and affection has a value and purpose all its own, not tarnished by the sexual overtures of perpetrators.

It may be initially difficult to trust those experiences of warmth. Fear may accompany them. We will need to share our feelings about them with therapists and sponsors. But in time we shall be able to enjoy genuine warmth for the gift it is to us.

The warmth of Your love is my heart's strong support.

Generosity is one of the fruits of a life committed to working the 12 Steps on a daily basis. It flows from a wellspring of serenity, gratitude and love. How different it is from the "giving" we were used to in incest, motivated by fear, shame and self-preservation!

Generosity flows from a basic attitude of trust towards the world, not to be mistaken for naivete. It is certainly not appropriate to *expect* oneself to be filled with it as a newcomer, or even after some time in the program. For generosity flows through us as a *gift* whose source is our Higher Power.

True generosity is possible when the giver has first been the recipient. In this 12-Step process we experienced the generosity of others to discover a valuable self beyond the stigma of incest. Generosity is an overflowing of the healing gifts we continue to receive.

I thank you for Your generous love.

No mother can be expected to love uncondi-tionally; each has her limitations. But no mother has the right to sexually abuse her offspring or fail to protect them from being harmed by oth-ers.

When we reach adulthood, there is only one person responsible enough to be our mother — ourself. Whether female or male, we can learn to be a caring non-abusive mother to our child within. Only then can we decide how we want to relate to the person we called "mother" when we were children. Perhaps the mothering side of ourself, who helped our inner child make it through the abuse, is the one who deserves tender, caring love this Mother's Day.

The earth is my true mother who gives me life.

For those of us who knew betrayal at the hands of our own parents, the search for home is one more of discovery than recovery. But why bother searching at all? If we have never known the home of our deepest longing, how can we even hope that it is attainable? Something at the depths of our being tells us we can.

That something at the center of our being people call God or "the true self." This is both the big secret and the paradox. After searching we come to find that our true home is deep within us. It is a peaceful loving union with our Higher Power. And the entranceway is through trusting relationships with others in which we are able to experience what it means to be loved and to love without a price tag.

Day by day I am coming home to myself.

Some of us mutilate ourselves because we believe we are "bad" and "shameful" persons.

The violence to our bodies includes anything we do to hurt ourself: stabbing, cutting, overdosing, burning, hitting, marathon running/walking/exercising/working. This has to stop. It may mean saying out loud, "It scares me to hurt myself, but it takes the edge off a deeper pain at least for the moment. I don't know what else to do. And I feel so ashamed."

Self-mutilation is isolating because it can scare, shock and disgust people. But let's face it. We have used it to distract ourselves from the betrayal of a child's trust by someone who ought to have been trustworthy. **The hurting can heal** if we are willing to do whatever it takes to stop hurting ourself.

The hurting must stop. Let it begin with me.

Even the most successful of us in the world harbor feelings of being a fake if we still carry the secret of our molestation.

No matter how much others affirm our goodness and lovability, down below lurk the feelings, "But they really do not know how disgusting I am." How can we go about regaining our own respect? How can we ever hope to look at the person in the mirror with love and acceptance?

We can begin by reaching out for help. We need to talk about what happened to us with someone who can help, someone with whom we can risk sharing our secret. This is the way to understanding, support and validation. This is the first step toward discovering we have been an acceptable, lovable person all along.

I am a lovable and worthwhile human being.

Just as "sham" and "shame" spring from the same linguistic root, they grow in us from the same root cause of incest. "Sham" is the false front we present to the world, hiding our inner "emptiness" and "worthlessness." "Shame" is our basic feeling that "I am a disgrace as a human being." In order to survive the betrayal of incest we assumed the blame for it. We became ashamed of who we are.

Shame is a double-bind imprisonment because to unlock its chains we need to share our secret. But to tell the truth about our feelings would be to admit our shame. And so the imprisonment continues. We need a lot of loving support to risk breaking out from the lies which prevent us from seeing that the shame of incest is the total responsibility of the perpetrator.

Help me break through the isolation of shame.

Many of us incest survivors are professionals used to helping others with their problems. We can feel vulnerable when we realize that we need healing support ourselves. When we first begin to struggle with the awareness that we are survivors, we can feel isolated.

Yet there is a higher percentage of survivors in the helping professions than in the general population. But the fear of breaking secrecy is tied in with the fear of losing professional anonymity and the cultural taboo against professionals having any perceived vulnerabilities. We still need help. Before we profess to helping others, we need to make a firm commitment to our personal healing.

I profess my faith in the healing process.

The strength of meetings comes from knowing we are not alone. When we go to meetings and listen to other survivors' stories, we find many points of identification with our own. In identifying with the sharing of others, we come to find that our own feelings are rooted in a real violation of our integrity.

The danger in going to meetings is when we start comparing ourself with others rather than identifying with their sharing. This leads to our separation from the group and the feeling that no one can really understand our own experience because it is different. This is self-deception.

The greatest gift we can personally receive in fellowships is to identify out of our own experience when another is sharing.

I identify with the shared feelings of others in order to break through the lies of isolation.

Choosing to work on our healing from incest by joining a 12-Step fellowship for survivors we find fulfillment from the time we begin taking the very first step in recovery.

Living the steps means more than attending meetings. At meetings we feel greatly relieved to discover that we no longer have to feel alone with incest. We identify with the shared feelings and experiences of other survivors and enjoy the fellowship and solidarity.

Healing requires a willingness to go to any lengths. Such a commitment means adopting a new spiritual way of living based on the 12 Steps. With a sponsor as our guide, regular Step meetings as our support and a Higher Power as our Source of this new life, we move into a deeper level of healing. Living the Steps transforms us from a bunch of "hard luck survivors" into "life thrivers."

I need the Steps in order to heal.

Being an incest victim means being subjected to the crisis of betrayal. Being a survivor means finding ways to cope with crisis without being obliterated by it. Finding a healed life beyond mere survival requires risk taking — including letting go of the feeling that life is normal only when we are in crisis.

Growing up in an incest atmosphere, many of us have become stuck in a crisis mode of functioning. We may not even feel alive unless we are dealing with some crisis.

Letting go of our state of constant crisis can be scary because it results in our having to face ourself and our feelings rather than some conflict external to us. Facing ourself and our feelings about the betrayal of trust is *the* healing crisis which, in time, will lead to a life of serenity.

Be my calm in the midst of crisis.

Leaving our body was a survival skill we developed during the abuse; that body being raped was not me. After a while leaving our body became automatic whenever we felt threatened. Later we weren't even aware of feeling threatened but found ourself leaving. Finally, we were unaware either of feeling threatened or leaving. It just happened.

Then we became scared because we had lost touch with bodily feelings and awarenesses and did not know how to regain them. We left our body originally to survive. Now it is time to start reconnecting in order to heal the split. We are encouraged to stay with it because it is a journey home.

I am coming home to my body.

Once we begin feeling our body again, migraine headaches, body memories, panic attacks, aches and pains, tremors and other such occurrences are commonplace. Basically, our body is calling ourself home in order to feel and release the past.

Feeling the rape as a child would have overwhelmed us. So we left our body. But it was still *our* body that was sexually violated and spiritually betrayed. So a major focus of the healing process is to re-enter, reconnect, feel and let go.

As we begin to feel our body and trust the feelings, we realize there is a lot of wisdom in our bodily feelings. Our body can tell us what feels safe and what is dangerous, when we have had enough — work, food, dealing with incest, etc. — and when it is time to rest, play or pray. We begin to trust that our Higher Power can give us guidance through bodily feelings.

Higher Power, help me to listen to the voice of my bodily feelings.

We have been brainwashed into believing that only death and destruction awaited us unless we stayed in darkness and secrecy!

Along with the betrayal of trust, the perpetrator implanted in us fear of what truly heals. But the healing rays of the sun — in other words, bringing the truth of our feelings and experiences into the light — will not destroy us, but free us.

When we move from the shade into the sun, we often have to take off some layers of clothing because we are warm. When we begin the healing process, we also begin letting go of some of the defenses that formerly cloaked and protected us. And that can be scary. Yet as we begin to take this risk in a warm, accepting, safe atmosphere (sunshine), we discover inner healing rather than fearful betrayal.

I choose to walk in healing sunshine.

Let's call incest what it really is: attempted murder of the human spirit. It was not a sexual act of little consequence. Rather, sexual violence and manipulation were the means used to betray our integrity.

Some victims of incest never survive the initial violence. Many others have committed suicide later, seeing no other way out of the constant terror and despair. And some of us have survived.

At those times when death seems like the only possible means of relief, we need to claim our worth. The perpetrators tried to kill our spirits, but we do not have to let them succeed. The attempted murder of a child by a trusted family member is what we still struggle with one day at a time. Our spirits are strong!

Higher Power, You have given me a spirit stronger than death.

It is not easy to say "I hurt" once we have experienced the betrayal of incest. Who can be trusted not to betray us in our vulnerability? Perhaps it is easier to numb out than to be in touch with our wound — our need for healing, for others, for love.

In finding others who genuinely care about us as human beings — which we do in 12-Step survivor fellowships — we gain the courage to risk saying, "I hurt." And we allow ourself to feel our vulnerability in the presence of caring people without being betrayed. In one sense we may be allowing ourself to feel more pain than we ever have. But underlying our pain is the hope of healing.

You can change my mourning into dancing.

A corollary to a well-known slogan in the 12-Step program, especially important for survivors of incest, goes: "But you can't give what you haven't got."

Unless we are able to receive the grace of healthy self-love, acceptance and hope, we are unable to truly help others. There are many helping professionals (or "amateurs") who are really trying to rescue themselves under the guise of helping others. While advocacy is an extremely valuable gift when practiced as part of Step 12, it will be a folly for our own spiritual well-being if we engage in it before attempting to integrate the 11 previous Steps of the healing process.

Lifegiving service is a gift that flows from the heart of one who has first received the grace of unconditional love and validation grounded in a reality greater than ourself.

May I share the gift of love and acceptance which I have received.

Like any other people, survivors of incest choose to have children or not. Sometimes our choices are guided by need: "I need to love a child in the way I never received love." Sometimes our choices are guided by myth: "I am afraid to have children because people say abuse survivors become child abusers."

We *can* become very loving parents if we remember that no matter how old we are, our own "inner child" needs continuing love, care, listening, patience and understanding from us.

For some of us, our own inner child is all we want to have. Others choose to bear and raise children with a partner or to adopt or take in foster children. Loving, nurturing, sustaining parents recognize that our first and last responsibility is to our inner child. From this relationship centered in a Higher Power flows all truly generative parenting.

Higher Power, I entrust the vulnerability of my inner child to Your care as well as my own.

Words do not suffice to describe the fear and anxiety associated with phobias for a person who has not experienced it. Sexual abuse survivors constantly live with the threat of such fear. It is a fear which is devastating and paralyzing, which can strike without warning when everything is going great. We feel as though our life is falling apart.

We cannot recover from phobias on our own; we need professional help. Enduring them alone might be submitting to a form of revictimization. A caring therapist and phone calls to supportive survivors can help us through the rough spots. Externalizing the energy otherwise directed against ourself in fear can also help. We need not go it all alone.

Fear overwhelms me; we conquer fear.

If we are not a success at everything we attempt, then we must be a failure. If we cannot be the perfect little girl/boy at all times, then not only will we be abused but we probably deserve it!

This "all-or-nothing" thinking once served as a means of survival in a world which was invading and overwhelming us. Now that we have survived to adulthood it is time to realize that all-or-nothing thinking is no longer in our best interest.

The long form of the Serenity Prayer used in many 12-Step groups talks about being "reasonably happy" in life as a realistic goal. Maybe we do not have to live our life in constant ecstasy or depression. Life has its ups and downs. Perhaps just for today we can accept ourself as an imperfect human being about whom we feel reasonably happy.

Higher Power, grant me neither the extremes of everything nor nothingness — only what I need today to live in reasonable happiness.

Often we feel our body betrayed us when we were sexually violated.

Body size, however, is something over which we have a measure of control. We can try to disappear by making ourself as thin and unobtrusive as possible. Or we might gain a lot of weight. We may believe that we *need* to be thin or fat or shapeless in order not to invite abuse. We assume responsibility for another's actions toward us.

But our body size did not cause our abuse. If we are still trying to regain some degree of personal control over our life by starving, purging or otherwise manipulating and abusing our own body, we must get help immediately. We do not deserve to destroy ourself; we deserve to be comfortable in our body. Most important, we need to treat our body with respect no matter what we feel about our physical self right now.

Your love heals both the shamed and the defiant body.

In setting out to create a work of beauty and functional excellence, one would look for both quality tools and a person who knew how to use them skillfully.

That is what recovery in 12-Step survivor groups is about. We enter deeply wounded, but with the strength of having survived a terrible betrayal. What our program of recovery offers us is guidance in getting to know the gifted Artist and Craftsperson within (Higher Power) along with quality tools with which to fashion a renewed life.

The most basic of the tools are the 12 Steps. The other tools which can be helpful along the way include survivor meetings, literature, the telephone, prayer and meditation, the slogans, journaling, affirmations, cuddlies and advocacy.

The best of tools only work if I use them properly.

During a sensory flashback one or more of our senses reminds us of when we were being abused. We may suddenly feel sick at the smell of a certain cologne, cringe at the sound of a door slowly opening or panic at the sight of certain-colored clothing. These put us back into the body of a vulnerable person under attack.

Sensory flashbacks are frightening because suddenly we are out of control and *feel* as though we are being abused again. In processing these experiences it is important to remember that we are not being revictimized. Rather, our body is re-presenting our whole person with this sensory experience in order to make it real for us so we can let it go and continue to heal.

My sight, hearing, taste, touch and smell remember, let go, and heal.

Emotional flashbacks involve reliving the feelings of being attacked, usually without memories connecting our emotions to a specific incident. We find ourself enraged all of a sudden, seemingly without provocation or crying with the voice of a young child.

Sometimes emotions and mental pictures may come to us separately. But they will come together over time if needed in order to heal.

There is a certain wisdom to the remembering process which is out of our conscious control. If we try to remain open to our Higher Power, trust what is happening, get the support we need, and not try to force memories to the surface, emotional flashbacks will begin to decrease and emotional integration to grow.

Higher Power, I trust You to allow me to feel today whatever I need to feel.

No matter how much we accomplish, we cannot erase the fact of the incest experience.

At the threat of realizing this, some of us are drawn to greater accomplishments. Others never live up to our potential. To our inner self, each success feels hollow, demanding we achieve more. Meanwhile, every failure or possibility of failure "proves" to us our worthlessness.

In recovery we begin to set our sights on a different type of achieving. We desire to live one day at a time in relative sanity under the guidance of a loving Higher Power. We are learning to tap into a new Source which does not rely on our achievements to find happiness in life.

You are accomplishing in me that which I am unable to achieve all alone.

Society's myth claims that abused children grow up to become child abusers. This is true insofar as most of us grow up to become *inner child abusers* without the *healing* of our damaged spirits.

Because as children we were offered strictly conditional, abusive "love," we may not even know how to love the child within. We are inner child abusers if we are alcoholic, eating disordered, workaholic, self-berating or cut off from our feelings.

The adult side of ourself may not like the fear, temper tantrums and spontaneous feelings or demands of our inner child. But stifling our inner child only perpetuates the cycle of violence and child abuse. We need to love and nurture our inner child on a daily basis.

Children have the right to be seen and heard and fully respected as valuable and vulnerable persons.

Sexual abuse of children is one of the most disaffirming acts of cruelty known to the human race. In most instances, children who survive such a trauma do so at the cost of knowing they are intrinsically lovable, worthwhile, valuable, good.

However, there is hope. We cannot relive our childhood years in a family which respects and cherishes us as we are. But we can live today with an attitude that affirms and values our inner child. We can turn degradation into affirmation.

Any positive self-statement repeated whenever negative thinking begins to overcome us is an affirmation of our person and helps counter some of the destructive impact of abuse. Initially affirmations may feel awkward. But we need to practice such truth-saying on a daily basis and affirm the goodness of our being.

I affirm the goodness of my being.

157

To be human means to come from the earth, from nature. How much are we in touch with it?

No human being, especially a child or vulnerable adult, should be subjected to the betrayal of incest. We were. Does that mean we are not recognizably human?

The betrayal of incest leaves us with many unanswered questions about our personhood. We will not find satisfying answers if we look to our perpetrators. If *they* knew what it really meant to be human, they would never have abused us. We need to find answers that are grounded in our true nature (of earth) and orient us to something greater than our own limitations (a Higher Power). Somewhere between the two stands the reality of our human nature.

Higher Power, help me to love and respect my human nature which is of earth and of God.

There is a proven, workable plan geared to meet the worst or the best life has to offer. It has helped millions of alcoholics, addicts, compulsive persons and those suffering in a variety of ways. It is also helping persons who were the victims of others' compulsions, addictions and criminal actions. It is called the 24-hour plan.

Its basic premise is that there is nothing life may deal out that a person and one's Higher Power cannot handle for 24 hours. When flashbacks, fears or unhealthy guilt set in, our minds can deceive us with the lie which is a repetition of the abuse: "You will always suffer this way." The 24-hour plan is our antidote to this lie until we realize the truth "This too shall pass." In a very real way, today (these 24 hours) is all we have.

May I use these 24 hours to live in Your love.

This word connotes an overly high opinion of oneself bordering on arrogance or a healthy sense of dignity and self-respect. In the first instance, pride can be worn as a defensive mask to conceal an inner sense of personal shame. In the second, it can be the mark of a person unburdened by unhealthy shame and guilt.

To say one is too proud to admit a history of sexual victimization is a thinly veiled way of saying, "I feel too ashamed to look at and accept my past." We survivors cannot afford this type of pride because it locks us more firmly into the victim role and allows perpetrators to remain unopposed. Such pride is nothing but denial mislabeled self-respect.

Allowing our inner feelings of shame and guilt to surface and be re-examined in a healing light helps us to replace false pride with true love of self.

May false pride not block my healing path.

The science of psychology calls rationalizing a defense mechanism. Psychotherapists can help their clients become aware of defense mechanisms that impede healthy relationships today. But before we learn to let go of our rationalizations, we ought to honor ourself for whatever ego integrity we were able to maintain while trying to make sense out of the most cruel and senseless of crimes.

We had good reason to rationalize our abuse — to explain it as somehow being okay. Doing that helped us to endure and survive. We have good reason to let go of our rationalizations today, to accept the truth of what happened, perhaps without knowing why. Doing so can lead to a new freedom to thrive in life. And isn't that the meaning we have been seeking all along?

Help me find the safe place to make sense.

Incest survival often involves enduring multiple personalities, flashbacks, panic attacks, compulsive behaviors, sleep disturbances or other consequences of traumatic abuse. But it is not mental illness.

Institutional psychiatric treatment, geared toward management and caretaking rather than caring and cure, holds little hope of healing for incest survivors. We may need to explore various healing/therapeutic modalities with professionals and peers who can walk the healing journey with us. But it is vital to know that our survival choices of the past were not choices of the mentally incompetent, but those of creative, vulnerable persons who can now make new choices to continue to survive, heal and thrive.

Surviving incest is a sign of mental strength, not mental illness.

Because one of the most long-lasting and pervasive effects of incest is a sense of personal isolation, it is important for us to identify and maintain a lifeline to recovery. A lifeline is like an umbilical cord connecting us to the Source of healing and life — our Higher Power, supportive survivors and an inner sense of self-worth and validation.

Perhaps knowing that we are not alone is the strongest aspect of our lifeline. It assures us we are connected with other survivors who are taking similar risks of growth and interaction in the world.

No matter where we are, we can connect with a Center whose unselfish love is greater than the power of abuse. Our lifeline helps us find the courage to live as unique individuals in the world by maintaining healing connections with others.

No matter where I am, I remain connected with the Source of life.

Prayer does not have to be seen as something so mysterious that it belongs only to the pious or people of religion. Nor need it be abused as it has often been by perpetrators who excuse their actions by calling themselves "persons of prayer" who are doing "God's will." In order for prayer to be lifegiving, it has to be both personal and interpersonal.

Personalizing prayer means not only do we call upon a Source we cannot see, but we reach out to others with whom we can relate in daily life. Many in the 12-Step program get down on our knees in the morning to ask for guidance and again at night to give thanks. We are also willing to personalize that prayer during the day when we are in need by reaching out to a supportive other with the request: "Help me."

May I personalize my daily prayer by reaching out to support others.

Attitudes which predispose us to revictimization are those rooted in negativity, which cut off all hope and trust in others. Lifegiving attitudes are based on prudent risk, vulnerability and trust in a Higher Power and in a world oriented toward life and growth.

Once abused, it is not easy to live by positive attitudes. The world can seem a dark, dangerous, unjust place where the innocent are victimized.

Recovery means saying no to negative attitudes based on fear, distrust and oppression. Recovery is having the courage to develop attitudes of love, nurturance and adequate protection for the innocent. Healing attitudes break the bonds of imprisoning violence. Healing attitudes give life.

———————

My basic attitude is one of openness to healing and growth on a daily basis.

While many of us believe incest recovery to be a lifelong activity, engaged in one day at a time, real improvement and health begin to come about in a relatively short time for those willing to commit to a healing program.

Trust and patience go hand-in-hand. If we do not see immediate results, we may distrust the process. At such times it is important to recognize that impatience with ourself and demands that we get better "all at once" are forms of self-abuse. We do not have to heap abuse upon abuse by being impatient with ourself.

Patience is a form of self-acceptance. It is a willingness to trust that we are where we are supposed to be right now and are progressing as we are supposed to progress — as long as we are doing the "footwork" of recovery and trusting in our Higher Power.

Be patient — God is not done with me yet.

If rage or hatred were all some of us felt toward "father," that would be easy. But how do we deal with those other feelings we may have of love, tenderness or sorrow? Like the rest of our life, our feelings toward father — even an abusive one — are often a mixed bag.

We can pretend that Father's Day is not on the calendar or say that a person who would sexually abuse a child cannot be called a father. We might say we detest the crime but love our father. A lot of feelings may be touched in us on Father's Day, but none comes easy or without pain, struggle and personal cost to us. The best gift we can give ourself in the midst of it all is to accept our feelings and seek out the support and love we need to live.

I can be a loving father to the orphaned child within.

Perhaps the reason so many of us are into constant "doing" is that a moving target is harder to hit (rape). Or maybe that nobody did *for* us as much as *to* us as children. Maybe we are trying to prove that we are okay after all. None of this will change our past history.

It is true that we can avoid facing ourself to some degree by keeping busy. But is it worth avoiding the feelings of pain, hurt and rage for the moment only to have them always relentlessly pursuing us? If doing a lot is a distraction from facing life, we are really "doing ourself in."

Doing has to flow from being. In other words, it is far more lifegiving to say, "What I do flows from who I am" than "I am what I do."

May what I do be in the service of life and of love.

Unconditional love cherishes another's being. In its pure form we can only find it from the Source of love — the best sense of whom people mean when they say "God." But even we flawed and wounded humans can cherish, love and respect a person's being without doing it violence. The belief in the possibility of this makes healing from sexual abuse a realistic hope.

Healing is about learning to respect, cherish and value our own being. The part of us who needs this love most is the child who did not receive it when growing up. This inner child is the very essence of ourself we come to know at the core of our being. Coming to know and love the child within is a process that leads us to cherish our being and to celebrate our existence.

_____

Teach me to cherish the child who is the heart of my being.

Feeling overwhelmed is common to incest survivors and not limited to our feelings around incest.

We can feel overwhelmed in other areas of life which at first glance do not appear to be related to incest. We may busy ourself with so much work or responsibility that we feel overwhelmed. We may feel overwhelmed by the expectations of others in relationship with us. We may feel overwhelmed when having options in life — ranging from choice of vocation to purchase of a personal computer.

Tools to employ when feeling overwhelmed include meditation and outreach. We do not have to go through this all alone; ask for help from a supportive other. We do not have to do everything at once; let go of what we cannot accomplish today and let today's work be enough. Bottom line when feeling overwhelmed: This too shall pass.

One day, one step at a time, I am okay.

"It gets better" are three reassuring words we need to hear when surviving incest does not seem to be worth it. Our program sponsor will likely confront us with them when we are ready to throw in the towel. And because that person has been through the hell of incest and is okay today, we do feel understood, reassured.

It gets better, but not always easier. If we have been in the healing process for a while, we know that in some ways it gets worse (feeling-wise) before it gets better. But we can also testify that it *has* got better for us. And that is part of our own inner reassurance we can hold to on days when everything feels like it is back to square one.

It gets better. That is the hope we cling to when we are being harassed by flashbacks, panic attacks, nightmares or nameless fears.

It gets better.

They said we were seductive as children. They tried to convince us that a little person, a vulnerable person, *made* the parent or another person in a position of power do what they did not intend to do!

People who perpetrate incest tend to perpetuate abuse. The perpetrators were in a position of power and responsibility — and misused it. They did not have the right to molest or rape us. They did not have the right to revictimize us by saying it was our fault — that we were seductive. But they did it.

In the past we may have felt we had to protect our abuser. We do not have to do so now. It was not our fault. Children and vulnerable adults are not to be blamed for the incest committed against them. The responsibility for incest belongs to the abuser.

I was innocent, not seductive.

Yucky and Icky will often be found in the vocabulary of children who have been abused. As children we experienced unwanted "icky stuff" on us or in us and being forced to do "yucky things." It may not be technical language, but it does touch directly on our felt experience.

Those feelings are still with us. We do not like to think about them or to feel them, because it feels "yucky" and "icky" all over again.

We who have grown into adulthood may have left those descriptive adjectives behind, but our inner child is often feeling yucky or icky. That child needs a loving person who will accept her or him no matter how she or he feels. Yucky experiences do not have to victimize us again. Icky stuff need not stick to us forever. With love and concern we can be cleansed of them.

Do not abandon me when I feel all yucky inside and icky outside.

While healing is definitely a process of life, strength and integration, we may sometimes feel that "all health is breaking loose."

This is not meant to be a cute pun but a serious warning. Some aspects of the healing process can leave us feeling worse *temporarily,* but they are not to be avoided. It hurts terribly to believe that trusted adults abused their responsibility and "love" for us. It can be heart-rending and gut-wrenching to re-experience the feelings of hurt, betrayal, rage and grief in the process of letting them go. But that is part of the healing process.

When healthy feelings and attitudes begin to break free within us, it can be very scary and painful. However, this time we will not be re-victimized because we are taking the steps to provide a safe and loving environment in which we choose to live.

Please keep on loving me when all health breaks loose.

There are so many ways to regret the past. In denial we regretted our behavior that "caused" our abuse. Later we regretted that the perpetrators chose to abuse us instead of nurturing us.

We do not have to regret the past, or idealize it. If we want to grow, all we have to do is accept it. Acceptance means letting go even of regrets that it could not have been otherwise. The past was what it was — and for us that included our being violated and abused.

Letting go of the past by accepting the horrors of its reality does not come without personal suffering and loss. However, it is not a death-dealing loss, but one in the service of new life. And we healing survivors do not regret that at all.

God, grant me the serenity to accept the things I cannot change.

Why are the relationships we so deeply need, the things in life which frighten us the most?

We can be quite clever about getting along with people, charming them, even gaining their respect and affection. But why do they still scare us?

Because we are incest survivors. And what it took to survive is different from what it takes to live and to thrive. Getting better does not mean we will never be afraid of people again. It means fear of people will no longer have to control our lives and prevent us from being ourselves. Getting better is learning gradually to replace fear of others with trust and love. It takes time.

———————

God, I need You to help me overcome my paralyzing fear of people, my fear of You.

Many are the times we have pulled out the "family album" of recollections to show others what a good family we had. Many of us can point to some good, happy, loving times.

The photos that make it to the family album, however, often are the ones which are posed. So was our life to the world outside. We kept the secret.

"This is my family," the child-in-the-adult says, pointing to the happy pictures that cannot erase the pain. "This is my family, too" are the flashback images which bring the much more horrifying pictures to light. "This was my family" is the sorrowing/healing acceptance of the family reality of the past which no longer has to control our present life.

I cannot get what I need to live from my family of origin; I trust in a Higher Power.

Sometimes it is very appropriate to call for help. Our fellowships of recovery are built upon that premise. We ask help from our Higher Power. We reach out for support by going to meetings. We share our feelings, struggles and joys with a caring therapist, understanding sponsor and supportive fellow survivors.

The basic message of recovery is that we cannot do it alone nor do we have to. Abuse taught us the lie that it is too dangerous to call for help.

But there is no longer the same risk in asking for help today — though we may still feel so. We have both the right and the need to ask for help. And if we are persistent, our cries will be heard by the growing number of survivor advocates and support networks who really care.

It is okay to ask for help.

Can anyone who grew up in a childhood "home" with so much tension, fear and abuse ever know peace? Yes. We shall know peace. "We Shall Know Peace" is part of The Promises (found in the "Big Book" of *Alcoholics Anonymous*) made to those who are willing to adopt a spiritual way of living through the 12 Steps.

The 12 Steps help us to accept the past, not without feeling, but without denial or that unhealthy clinging called resentment. They guide us to an honest appraisal of ourself and our past relationships while helping us to find lifegiving, spiritually nurturing choices in the present. They mark out a path that helps us find the peace for which we so deeply long.

We shall know peace.

While the intense pain associated with our victimization helped motivate us to seek a more spiritually self-caring way of life, we can slip back into old patterns of self-neglect once life becomes more "normal" or "calm." Maintaining spirituality is our key to insuring that we will forget neither where we have come from nor the importance of living sanely and serenely today.

Our spiritual side needs to be fed, nurtured, exercised, challenged and rested on a daily basis as surely as our physical and emotional sides do. Daily spiritual maintenance thwarts the recurrence of dis-ease and promotes spiritual wellness.

In maintaining wellness I need daily spiritual food, play, work, exercise and rest.

Somewhere between deprivation and over-abundance is the balance called "enough." Do not ask unhealed incest survivors what that is because we only know extremes.

Enough is a safe place where we do not have to fear being abused. Enough is dealing with life as it comes, one day at a time. Enough is being able to trust in an Inner Guide and in outer supports. Enough is knowing it is just too scary sometimes to trust at all — and then prudently risk trusting anyway.

Enough is receiving success without the certainty that abuse is about to follow. Enough is enduring personal failures without believing we are failures at being persons. Enough is the willingness to believe that individually and together we have the capacity to live, to love, to grow in healing and grace.

Higher Power, You are my Enough.

The goal of the healing process might be seen more in terms of completion rather than perfection. To be complete is to have everything we need in order to live life for today. This includes flaws and imperfections as well as gifts and strengths.

Unlike perfection (which stresses flawlessness), completion says we can heal because we already have all the tools we need — within ourselves and for the asking from a Higher Power and fellow survivors. Completion is the stuff of real life; perfection is of fantasy. We heal by learning to live in the real world.

Perfection sees us locked into the role of victim; completion engages us in a process from victim to survivor to thriver. Perfection lives in a fantasy future of trouble-free living; completion focuses on today which has troubles and joys of its own.

I have everything I need to heal; Higher Power, show me the way.

How can we ever trust a power greater than ourselves when as helpless children we were devastated by abusers whom we had trusted? How can we believe in a loving God when those who professed to love us betrayed our love by active abuse or silent denial of the crime?

We were betrayed and it hurts to feel it. But feel it we must. And express it we must — in good time and with people we feel safe with. We honor ourselves by externalizing our feelings of betrayal by God, by parents, by people who violated our trust and integrity.

When the feelings of betrayal arise, we do not betray ourselves by denying them. We reverence ourselves by accepting the hurt, confusion and rage of our inner child who knows we are valuable and deserving of care and respect.

I am precious.

Understanding, literally, would mean to "stand under" others and support them with the strength of our person. Many of us tried to be understanding children towards our abusers when we were much too young to support them. Many of us have grown into adults who put aside our needs in order to be understanding towards others.

In recovery we learn that *we* are important enough persons to be understood. Our needs, cares and concerns matter to a loving Higher Power who has been understanding us even when we felt we didn't deserve it.

What is important in our recovery is that we use the tools our Higher Power gives us to receive the understanding we need to thrive and to flourish.

God understands me at all times.

Many of us can remember a time when sugar, alcohol or other drugs took the edge off the fear and panic that always lurked just below the surface of our awareness. But the relief was only temporary, and in time we realized our "remedy" was only inflicting more abuse on us.

When we continue to indulge in substance abuse, our out-of-focus feelings loom dark and threatening. When we abstain one day at a time, long-repressed and often disturbing feelings begin to resurface.

Recovery means working the tools and steps of a fellowship that deals with our addiction as well as a 12-Step fellowship for incest survivors. In these complementary recovery programs we learn to let go of abuse and grow in loving self-respect.

I treat myself with love and respect.

Initially surviving meant enduring the trauma of our victimization until we were able to escape that imprisonment. Moving away from an abusive environment was an important step on our way to freedom.

While this external freedom was vital, it did not guarantee our emotional freedom. Working the steps and sharing with other survivors is a pathway to freedom from the fear, guilt and confusion implanted in us by our abusers. We learn that the victim role was a cruel imposition on our true nature.

Recovery means letting go of a lifestyle of victimization and embracing the way of surviving and thriving. We are free to assume responsibility for our own lives and accept the guidance of a loving Higher Power. Day by day we grow in freedom and serenity.

I am free to be me.

There was a time when we felt out-of-place and "bad" in a hush-hush world where even the judicial system made our victimization feel like a crime *we* had committed.

Some of us walked around with eyes and shoulders lowered, afraid that everyone could read the secret held in our bodies. At other times an erect, stiff, defiant posture became our way of challenging a world which we felt had betrayed and rejected us.

Today we are learning to let go of fear and shame and opening to love and reverence. We can stand comfortably at our full height, muscles relaxed, eyes meeting the world of which we are a part. Standing tall means saying yes to ourselves and the universe and no to those who abuse the precious gift of life.

I am part of a loving universe.

Many incest survivors suffer from eating disorders such as anorexia, bulimia or compulsive overeating. That which is meant for our bodily nourishment becomes a means of our daily destruction!

Recovery from our eating disorders begins when we are able to admit we are powerless over food, life has become unmanageable for us and God can and will lift our obsession. The 12-Step program of Overeaters Anonymous (OA) is one such fellowship in which we find help.

Eating disorders isolate us; recovery teaches us to personalize our prayer. That means going to a meeting or calling another flesh-and-blood person to say "Help me." Our experience is that God can and will, if sought.

I trust in You, O God.

It gets better. No matter where we are in the healing process, we need to hold on to the hope of recovery and of life beyond incest. Associating with other survivors who are now thriving serves as a living reminder of this hope.

Initially, it can be very distressing, even agonizing to re-experience the memories of our abuse. Yet even this is a process of acceptance by means of which we learn to stop torturing ourselves and to respect the feelings of our inner child without judgment.

Hope is an inner strength which links us with our Higher Power and enables us to focus on what is most meaningful for us in life. Hope frees us from the old tapes which our perpetrators implanted and opens us to the source of universal loving energy within, whom many of us call God.

I place my hope in God.

Resting near the calm of the ocean on a hot summer's day has a way of soothing and refreshing one's spirit. Through meditation and visualization we can take such a nurturing vacation no matter where we are or what the season. We who have known disturbing inward journeys (flashbacks) all the more need such a healing voyage.

We need do no more than find a quiet time and place, close our eyes and be transported to this tranquil scene. How we enjoy the scene is up to us.

When we are able to tap such resources of peace, tranquility and healing within ourselves, we become empowered. We realize that soothing contact with our Higher Power can be as close as our next meditation. We learn that serenity is not something we need to chase after, but is a way of life deep within our spirits.

You are my refreshment.

Incest isolates. Our victimization left us feeling alone and "different" in our family of origin. We often found ourselves unable to tell others outside the family about it or were not believed when we did. We didn't understand how a loving God could let this happen to us unless we were really "bad" persons. Relationship with people the same sex as our abusers could repulse us. Rarely did real intimacy seem possible.

The process of recovery invites us into relationship with a Higher Power, a sponsor, same sex survivor groups and women and men recovering together. As others help validate our experience through sharing, we find ourselves letting go of isolation and learning to relate in healthy ways.

Incest had isolated us from ourself. In recovery we learn to accept ourselves as we are.

Together we can.

As victims, "today" was a time that did not exist for us. Yesterdays held us bound in fear, hurt, guilt and resentment. Tomorrows seemed like false hopes which never arrived. And we felt powerless to live for today in a healthy, responsible manner.

In recovery we realize that today is all we have. Because we have survived our incestuous pasts, we have the opportunity to live for today as victims no more. The gift of life today is there for our choosing through the grace of our Higher Power and with the support of our program.

Recovery is a process that takes place in the here-and-now. Living in the present opens us to life with its pains and its joys.

Thank You for the gift of today.

We survivors have been carrying a heavy load for many years. Our emotions, spirits and even our bodies have become contorted under the heavy stress of the incest experience. Maybe we never knew we had the right to put it down. Or maybe we have been afraid to. So we held on.

Those of us who have come into program deserve congratulations for our courage. We also deserve to put down the burden we should never have had to carry. Yes, it will hurt because we have been carrying it for a long, long time. But in 12-Step we are among others who have walked a similar road. They offer us their experience, strength and hope in moving from holding on to letting go.

I am in a safe place.

It was our holding on that left us stuck in a rut of victimization — feeling all alone, isolated and constantly on the defensive. Letting go is a choice we make on our own behalf. We choose to let go into life, into a natural world that welcomes us, into our own true nature.

It can be frightening to let go of the familiar. So we don't have to let go all at once. We can let go little by little, one day at a time. Today we may choose to let go enough to smell the beauty of a rose. Or perhaps we may ask for a hug from someone who genuinely cares for us and respects our boundaries. The more open-handed we become, the more open our hearts are to receive life's gifts.

I open my heart to receive.

"Let go and let God" is a slogan that has withstood the test of time in various 12-Step programs. It means that we do not let go into the power of persons, places or situations that will end up victimizing us again. Instead, we let ourselves go into the care and guidance of a loving God.

Let go *and* let God is the pathway to healing. This can be scary for those of us who believed in a God very much in the image of our abusers. Through the support and care of our fellowship of recovery, we begin to develop a healthy, life-giving notion of a Higher Power. This under-standing helps free us from emotional dependency upon unhealthy persons and opens us to a trusting relationship with a loving Higher Power who will not betray us.

Let go and let God.

Healing is a life-renewing and lifegiving process that addresses our wounds in the context of
our whole person. No matter how badly we
have been hurt, our wounds never become all
we are, nor are they the only object of our
healing; our whole person is. Healing addresses
our "brokenness," yes, but always remembering
our wholeness.

As scars and memories are a part of healing,
so is new strength and courage. Surviving is a
vital part of healing and it can lead to thriving.
Healing does not bring us back to the way of
living we had before our abuse. It leads us to
integrity and wholeness through which we can
live our lives today. Healing is not a "thing" that
repairs, fixes or glues us together. Healing is a
continuing process which deepens, expands and
opens us to life.

I am in a daily process of healing.

Caretaking is one of the ways we behave in order to avoid dealing with our own needs and feelings.

Caretaking is a behavior many of us learned as young children in a dysfunctional family. Emotionally immature adults (who were often our abusers as well) depended on us to assume adult responsibilities. We learned that we were expected to be caretakers and that others needed us to take care of them.

Recovery means letting go of caretaking and accepting responsibility for our own lives. In the process we may feel cheated out of our childhood and resentful toward those who led us to believe our only choice in life was caretaking. Expressing, sharing and releasing these feelings is the gateway to freedom. We give the world back to God and accept responsibility for one life only — our own.

God, grant me the willingness to accept responsibility for my own life.

What AAs have long called "the 13th Step" is a dangerous misuse of program to initiate sexual relationships.

We are a vulnerable population. Some of us feel we don't have the right to say no to others' sexual advances. We *have* the right and the responsibility to ourselves to do this. Others long for a partner who will love and accept us without abusing us. We need to realize that people in program are at different levels of emotional maturity and need.

12-Step anonymous fellowships provide a relatively safe and healthy environment for recovery. By committing ourselves to working the 12 Steps, we help establish an atmosphere that rules out "the 13th Step" in our fellowships.

Recovery is a 12-Step process.

Many of us would be appalled if we saw the harshness shown to others that we have often given ourselves. Beating ourselves up is unhealthy and unfair. We never deserved abuse and we certainly do not deserve it now. As creations of a loving Higher Power we deserve understanding, compassion and gentleness. In fact, they are the very sustenance of our life.

Taking time for meditation or a walk, treating ourselves with flowers or to a concert, working no more than we need to and playing more than we feel we should are examples of acts of kindness toward ourselves. Who of us would not treat a child with love and gentleness? Yet each of us has a child within in need of our love and compassion. Listen to the child within and respond with the open and gentle heart of a caring parent.

God, may I be gentle with myself.

Now that we no longer live in a threatening place, we need to learn to relax in order to heal our bodies overstressed from a life of tension and intensity. Breathing deeply relaxes our lungs and our spirits. Aerobic exercise releases stress and allows us to feel our life force flowing anew. Walking and swimming reconnect us with earth, air and water of which we are part. Aesthetic activities (art, music, poetry, etc.) relax our bodies as they open up our spirits. Meditation gradually opens us to inner calm and stillness. Play is wonderfully relaxing because it is free and spontaneous.

As we grow in our ability to let go, we begin to enjoy the feelings of a relaxed mind, body and spirit. We become more at home with ourselves and in our world.

Higher Power, grant me the spirit of relaxation.

We may continue to feel fear in response to some odors, sounds, tastes, touches, sights or for no reason. Often this is due to re-experiencing an aspect of a threatening situation in our history. The perpetrator is usually no longer present but fear remains. It is important to realize at such times that fear is just a feeling. Our abusers hurt us; the feeling of fear will not.

Breathe deeply, accept and acknowledge the fear we are feeling. Often it is felt most strongly by our inner child. If we are in a dangerous situation, make haste to remove ourselves. If it is a reminder of our abuse and our powerlessness, allow the feeling but also reassure our inner children that we will be okay. Love and tenderness directed towards ourselves and received from other survivors who understand our feelings are healing antidotes to fear.

God, heal my fear with Your love.

Only survivors ask, "Did it really happen to me?" Only someone who has undergone a severe trauma has to deal with the acceptance of its reality. We were raped, physically and emotionally violated, betrayed, invaded. So we have to deal with this question and the deeper one of life's meaning as persons who were innocent yet betrayed, overpowered and taken advantage of.

To admit that it happened is to allow ourselves to feel the pain of our betrayal and degradation as well as the loss of our fantasy family. But it is also to acknowledge that we have survived the devastation of incest. In doing so — and the struggle to do so can be ongoing — we claim for ourselves a healthy life beyond incest.

God, grant me the strength to acknowledge the truth of my past so that I may live more freely in the present.

The fantasy family is the one we may re-member having fun with, doing things together or being looked up to by others. It is a fantasy family not because positive experiences were not there, but because we may deny the effects of incest which were also present.

It is hard to let go of our fantasy family. If we weren't loved at all, we would never have been able to survive. Yet abuse was mixed in with whatever love we received. So we constructed one-sided fantasy families.

To let go of the fantasy family in our minds is to face the agony of our feelings so long pent up within: "How could they have said they loved me, then done this to me, an innocent child?" We need not face the agony alone. There is help. Reach out. We care.

I am not alone.

Many incest survivors struggle with physiological addictions to sugar, alcohol, narcotics, nicotine, caffeine, or behavioral addictions to gambling, work, spending, anxiety, sex, excitement, destructive relationships, and so forth. Those of us who are survivors and addicted know the inner longing for love, acceptance, well-being, "God".

Addictions lie. They tell us they can fill the gap, satisfy the longing, but they never do. On the contrary, addictions prevent us from being open-handed and open-hearted to receive the genuine love that is available for us. In working the steps with the support of others to deal with our addictions, we gain the serenity that comes from loving ourselves as we are and the courage to put down our addictions one day at a time.

God, grant me the courage to put down my addictions and take up Your will for me just for today.

By praying the first thing in the morning and last thing before going to sleep, we are better able to put life into proper perspective. We recall that we are powerless over the incest in our past and entrust ourselves in the present to the care of a Higher Power.

This is the only notion of "God" we need to start with. We may find it hard to pray if our notions of God are still tied to our abusers. Yet even if we cannot fully trust God, we remember that Step 3 calls for entrusting ourselves to the *care* of God — and not to abuse, punishment or manipulation.

Healthy relationships need time and attention in order to grow. "The daily double" has been a tried-and-true way for 12-Step people in achieving closer contact and a deeper relationship with our Higher Power.

I am Higher Powered!

There are two kinds of guilt. One is the awareness that we have *done* something wrong and need to make amends. The other tells us we *are* bad, unworthy people. The former leads to healthy living and relationships; the latter to beating up ourselves.

The 12 Steps (especially 4 through 10) are designed to deal with the first type of guilt which challenges us to grow. The second type only breeds self-hatred, resentment, compulsive behaviors and destructive life patterns.

In recovery we learn that unhealthy, false guilt has no place in our lives. When it arises in us we pray for the willingness to let it go, to turn it over to our Higher Power. Now we accept only the guilt that says we owe amends. Anything else is not recovery but continued victimization.

I am worthy.

Incest has caused us to become more anxious than we normally would have. Most people feel anxious in strange or new situations. But while others tend to relax in familiar surroundings, there is always a part of us that is on guard because we were violated and betrayed by the familiar (a family member or other person we were led to trust).

Anxiety serves us today when it alerts us to a potential danger so that we can respond with self-protection or by leaving a threatening environment. But holding onto anxiety is like clutching a former security blanket that only harms us now by overstressing our bodies and emotions. Praying for the willingness to let our anxiety go into the hands of God trades in unhelpful behavior for a new Higher-Powered security.

I rest secure in God.

Photographs are visual reminders that we are flesh-and-blood individuals deserving understanding, acceptance and nurturance as much as any other. Snapshots of ourself as children remind us that we were innocent, powerless and in no way responsible for our abuse. Looking at photos of ourselves can remind us that we are individuals with beautiful spirits.

Because the inner child is the most precious and vulnerable part of us, we may choose to carry a snapshot of ourself as a child in our wallet. Occasionally looking at this precious child opens our heart to the love and nurturance such a one needs to live and never got in the dysfunctional family. The child we can love most dearly is the child the photo reminds us we once were and who is still very much alive within us today.

You are my precious child.

The telephone is an important lifeline of recovery. When feelings threaten to overwhelm us or we are tempted to indulge in self-destructive behavior, when we are feeling good and want to share our joy, and even when nothing remarkable is happening in our life and feelings, the telephone is a valuable instrument for putting into practice the principles of recovery.

Incest often leaves us feeling alone, different, isolated. By means of the telephone, at any time, we can have a person-to-person survivors' meeting to bridge those feelings. And so every time we make a program call we say yes to surviving and no to continued victimization.

When we use the telephone as a regular part of our program, we are healing and reaching out to other survivors as well. We become double winners in recovery.

Reach out and survive.

When flashbacks and feelings about incest become intense, we can be inclined either to run away or to devote all our energies to working on them. "Easy does it" leads us through a middle ground of healing instead.

We learn to prioritize our needs and feelings — we don't ignore them or attack them headlong. Recovery is a lifelong process through which we learn to adopt an ease and gentleness towards ourself. We also take heart from other survivors whose experiences assure us that this too shall pass, and that life gets better.

Today is an opportunity to work our program in a sane and serene manner. Morning meditation helps give perspective to our day. Spot checks during the day remind us that *easy does it.* And our inventory at day's end calls us to give thanks for that which has been grace — another day of recovery.

Easy does it.

"I can't. God can. I'll let God" — goes the short version of the first three steps. In learning to turn things over to our Higher Power, we find that we are empowered by joining our will with God's, and so we can live life more freely and spontaneously.

Whenever an issue comes up over which we feel powerless, we learn to let go and let God. Freed from the burden of responsibility for life's outcome, we move from fear to freedom, from paralysis to action.

We need to turn over positive feelings too; otherwise, they can arouse an anxiety in us that we might try to ease with self-destructive behavior. Turning it over allows us to have feelings without being obsessed by them and to share our joys and struggles with other survivors and our Higher Power.

I can't. God can. I'll let God.

A tightness in our shoulders, a flutter in our stomach, a sudden shallowness of breathing — these are just a few of the many ways our bodies can be telling us we are experiencing feelings. In order to survive we often have ignored these signals. But now we are learning to care about ourselves enough to become aware of our bodily changes and the feelings they indicate.

Breathing slowly and more deeply can be one way of opening to our feelings. There are many ways.

Listening to our feelings does not mean being controlled by them. When we are able to listen to and dialogue with our feelings, we gain the freedom to respond (rather than react) to them. Listening to our feelings is a means of genuinely loving ourselves.

My feelings are a blessing.

We may have grown up judging all feelings to be bad and therefore tried to stay numb any way we could. Or else we might distrust a feeling of pleasure or forbid ourselves ever to experience anger. When we begin to allow ourselves to feel again (maybe for the first time in years) this too passes. Even our frozen resentment is our way of crying out "unfair!" — because it is unfair to be cut off from our feelings.

We will not forever feel in a panic, sad, terrified, angry. Nor will we feel continuous happiness or equilibrium. We are human. We change and we grow. Feelings are as waves of energy that pass through us. They do not make us bad or unworthy. They just tell us we are human and alive.

Feelings change.

How often we have hated ourselves for having a body that could be invaded, manipulated, abused! Often we have punished ourselves by constantly overtensing our muscles or overstressing our internal organs.

When we begin to make amends, various parts of our body (and our body as a whole) usually belong at the top of our list. Much more than saying "sorry," making amends is engaging in a mending (healing) process. We let go of old resentments against our body, begin to appreciate our physical being and how those parts have helped us survive, and enter into a new partnership with our body.

We now choose to relate to our whole body in a lifegiving manner. This, in turn, teaches us self-respect and limit setting. The more we love our body, the less likely we are to allow further abuse from ourself or others.

I love my body.

Many of us have come to find inner guidance from our Higher Power through that voice which speaks from the center of our being. This inner voice, which is always lifegiving, is found at the depths of our being in love and serenity and is variously called God, Higher Power, intuition, inner guide and so forth.

Our inner voice is best able to offer us guidance if we establish an open channel with it through daily meditation and if we willingly discuss the guidance it offers with our sponsor or spiritual advisor. Our inner voice will never deceive us.

Growing to trust our inner voice is an important way of turning our will and life over to the care of a loving God of our understanding. Doing so, we are empowered and freed from victimization to accept a fuller, happier life.

Thy will, not mine, be done.

Usually we choose persons to sponsor us whose recovery attracts us, who work the Steps daily and who are willing to share their personal experience, strength and hope with us. In trusting ourselves and our feelings with our sponsor and in receiving their acceptance and encouragement, we begin to value ourselves more as persons and to give ourselves the love and respect we previously may have sought indiscriminately from others.

A sponsor relationship teaches us we can be cared about without being betrayed, loved without becoming lovers and valued without payoffs (sexual or otherwise). By moving from a survivor to a thriver, in time we find that others ask us to become their sponsor. In this way we continue to pass on the gift we have so generously been given.

God, thank You for the gift of my sponsor.

"Let us love you until you are able to love yourself" is a healthy form of dependence in 12-Step recovery. In varying degrees we are dependent upon our program, group, sponsor and Higher Power as we learn to love and value ourselves.

This dependency is very different from the unhealthy dependency many of us previously had towards others. Here we allow ourselves to be dependent upon our Higher Power and our recovery program in order to grow to interdependence and responsibility.

In truth, no one is totally independent. In program, however, we learn that we have a measure of independence in setting personal boundaries, making life choices and deciding how we will relate to our world. A balance in sane and healthy interdependence is another gateway to freedom in living.

True freedom means interdependence.

A victim's no is not respected by the initiator of incest who employs physical or emotional power to make sure of that.

We who have moved from victims to survivors are learning to say no. Sometimes we feel we have to add explanations and justifications to our no-saying. But as our sponsors remind us, "No is a complete sentence." Learning to say no is a part of the normal development we were denied when we were told we did not have a right to our own lives, to our own bodies.

In recovery, learning to say no is an important step to gaining a fuller self-acceptance. It is also evidence of choice-making because we cannot say yes to ourselves without putting realistic limits on the demands of others. Saying no, then, is an important aspect of learning to choose the gift of self.

"No" is a complete sentence.

When we are able to let go of violent attitudes and behaviors toward ourselves, we create the space that makes love and healing possible. In a certain sense, this making space is itself the beginning of love.

We were not given a space that was valued nor were our boundaries respected. We were taught instead that love and violence went hand-in-hand. We did not know that love had very little to do with the crumbs of kindness our unhealthy families may have tossed us when we were not being violated.

Love is care without manipulation, nurturance without neediness and respect without deceit. In recovery program we commonly hear, "Let it begin with me." Today, each of us may choose to respond to ourself with acts of love filling the space in our lives where violence ends.

Let love begin with me.

Being powerless over our experiences of incest means that we cannot alter the fact of our abuse or its consequences for our lives today. However, in recovery program we learn that powerlessness is not helplessness. When combined with trust in a loving Higher Power, it makes it possible to let go of denial, rationalization and resentment in order to live life more freely and fully. Ironically, powerlessness understood thus is our key to real empowerment.

A helpless person cannot say no, cannot set limits, cannot make choices, can exist only in fear and paralysis. We who admit our powerlessness, conversely, ask a Higher Power for those needs we cannot provide for ourselves. We are discovering a way of becoming "Higher-Powered."

God, be my strength in weakness.

Reading literature written by other recovering incest survivors is one sure way of validating our feelings and experiences as well as fostering our own recovery. Read on a daily basis, this literature helps us to let go of personal isolation in order that we might find a real connection with other incest survivors. We are thereby challenged to live and grow.

Our daily readings reinforce our 12-Step program by reminding us to place the principles of recovery over the personality or opinions of any specific author.

Survivor literature helps us tap into our inner source of experience, strength and hope through hearing it shared by others. It can form a basis for daily reflection and meditation.

Higher Power, tell me what I need to hear today through my program readings.

The root meaning of intimacy is literally "into fear." For us survivors who learned to respond with fear to interpersonal closeness, the wisdom of recovery tells us that the only way out is through facing our fears.

Modern culture often equates intimacy with sexual relations, but that is only one possible expression. Many of us incest survivors who have had sexual intercourse forced on us in the name of "love" know it has nothing to do with intimacy. True intimacy is an openness to relationship that is spiritually based and involves our bodies and feelings as we choose to invest them.

Intimacy allows us to be truly at home with ourself. From this basis we are able to foster close and trusting relationships with God and others.

God, let me know my oneness with You.

It takes a lot of humility to work this program of recovery. It takes that aspect of humility called honesty for us to look at ourselves clearly and openmindedly so that we can face the truth about ourselves and our abusers. It also takes acceptance, the basis of humility, to claim ourselves as our own.

Humility is a candid acceptance of life on life's terms. It comes from the word "humus," meaning earth or soil. There's nothing like digging in a garden with our own hands to get in touch with reality, earthiness, life. So too, humility is an attitude that grounds us in the goodness of our natural life.

Humility is the opposite of denial and the antidote to the poison of incestuous secrecy. Thus, humility is an attitude and a virtue that gives life.

Humility is empowering.

Flashbacks and memories are not the only reminders of violation for some of us. There is also a wide array of physical effects of our abuse where there was bodily force involved. More subtle but nonetheless real and damaging are the long-term effects of internal stress, tension and pressure, which can manifest as high blood pressure, migraine headaches, glaucoma, chronically aching muscles and various respiratory and digestive problems.

We may be inclined to hate our bodies for bearing these reminders or become bitterly resentful toward those who harmed us. Getting the anger out toward our abusers is important so we can assert our value, decry the injustice and make space in ourself for the healing love of our Higher Power. Listen to the Higher Power speaking these words of love to us 24 hours a day:

"All I want for you is to enjoy My love."

As children in a dysfunctional family system we tried hard to be peacemaker or problem-solver, or to be as invisible as possible. But we weren't able to cure our unhealthy families or prevent our abuse. But that didn't stop us. In our minds we created the illusion that things might finally get better if only we tried harder! And on and on it went.

Just as our abuse wasn't stopped, so too our healing cannot be accomplished solely by self will. Healing calls for a spaciousness that trying hard does not allow. Love is that spaciousness. And it has nothing to do with trying hard and everything to do with receiving the gift of a Higher Power.

Love heals the wounds of violence.

Tomorrow is that mythical day which never arrives — the day when we will set our lives in order, stop abusing ourselves and really begin to live.

When we were children we may have lived in hope that tomorrow life would be more carefree and the abuse would stop. It never did. Perhaps deep down inside we still fear tomorrow will never come; life will never be better. But there is a remedy . . .

When we choose to live today and let tomorrow take care of itself, life becomes simpler. We might not always want to trust our Higher Power, but we could be willing to risk it for today. We might not always want to stop abusing ourselves or worrying about others, but we need not do either today. Sane living might be attainable for today with the help of our Higher Power.

Today is enough.

Taking a daily inventory is much less traumatic than trying to review the events of our whole life at once. We find we are no longer paralyzed by simple problems. We are also surprised to learn how active our Higher Power is in our mundane life. In fact, we begin experiencing our life as less overwhelming and more balanced and filled with hope and possibilities.

As we review our day, instances may come to mind where we may have been self-righteous or wronged another. This is an opportunity to pray for that person and to make amends. A daily personal inventory helps us to let go of old self-images often handed to us by abusers, and to receive a new, honest perspective of who we are in daily life.

Thank You, God, for the vision of myself.

When we act inappropriately or fail to act, we seek to make amends — to another, to ourself, to our Higher Power. We live in the present and respond to life out of who we are today. Sure the incest still affects us, but we do not confuse our abusers of the past with the healthier people we choose to associate with today.

Making amends is lifegiving because it restores balance to a relationship. Admitting we were wrong in the past may have been the opportunity for an abuser to take advantage of us. But doing so today in healthier relationships is a means of claiming power as we accept responsibility for our own actions (and no one else's).

Higher Power, continue to be a healing force in my relationships.

Living the Steps of recovery from the destruction of incest opens us to the grace of a spiritual awakening. While the words spiritual awakening might seem strange and mysterious, they are just a way of saying "waking up to life as it really is and as it can be for us today."

Having a spiritual awakening is coming to realize that there is a caring Higher Power to offer us support and guidance in life so that we might live in serenity and happiness. It means coming out of stifling, dark isolation and breathing deeply, feeling all our feelings and not being destroyed by them. A spiritual awakening involves the realization that sexual abuse is not the only fact of our lives and that we have a worth, beauty and potential far greater than our abusers ever led us to believe.

Every day I am more awake to life!

Clear thinking is one of the fruits of working our program of recovery. Being numb, confused or spaced out is now replaced with clarity, insight and perspective. Through daily living the 12 Steps we have gained a new clarity that allows us to assume responsibility for ourselves and no one else. We can make choices and set limits aware that we are never alone but have a loving Higher Power to guide us.

The pain, anger and loss that arise as our minds clear will not destroy us or anyone else but lead us to a new freedom to live life without the threat of further sexual abuse.

Higher Power, as my mind clears I see Your loving presence within and around me, and I am encouraged.

"Keep coming back" is a program slogan that has to do with perseverance in recovery even when it feels the devastating feelings may never end.

When we keep coming back we find that the intensity of our suffering subsides. We begin to experience new feelings of hope, enjoyment, satisfaction and serenity.

In the early stages of our recovery we may not know if healing is really attainable for us. But as we keep coming to meetings, find a sponsor, use the telephone and read the literature, we begin to gain hope and encouragement from the "winners" in the program. The winners are those who have kept coming back and have found a life of happiness and self-acceptance beyond the devastation of incest. We can become winners too, as long as we keep coming back!

Keep coming back.

It takes a lot of courage to make it through incest alive — much as it does through a war. Only in this war the survivors are mere children with no weapons to speak of. To proclaim ourselves survivors in a world that often does not want to hear it further attests to our courage.

Now that we are recovering from incest, we can use our courage to our advantage. First, we need to care for ourselves and live healthy lives. We may also reach out to other adult survivors who still suffer and feel alone. And we can become advocates for those who continue to be victimized.

Sometimes it takes a lot of courage just to get out of bed in the morning. But every time we act against fear and on behalf of our own recovery, we are demonstrating lifegiving courage.

I am courageous.

Even though we were in no way responsible for our abuse, the feelings that we could somehow prevent it by being better offered some of us hope in a desperate situation. And we survived! Far from being failures, we have proved to be successful at survival. Now that we are able to choose a safer environment in which to live, we need no longer label ourselves failures for crimes committed against us.

Today we succeed by valuing ourselves, by choosing life and recovery, and by becoming the healed and whole persons we were meant to be. We succeed by living in the present without denying our past. We succeed by avoiding violence against ourselves and others. Our very living and breathing is our most basic testimony to success against the violence and oppression of our abusers.

May I not fail to see today how lovable and worthwhile I am.

In the past, looking at our lives was something we avoided because we were convinced that we were far from perfect. In recovery we have come to see ourselves as lovable human beings with a combination of virtues and character defects. When working the Steps we grow in the conviction that our Higher Power will remove our defects of character as needed for our growth and healing. They do not disappear like magic, but are lifted on a daily basis as we begin to live healthier lives.

"Progress, not perfection," means beginning to live life on life's terms and taking responsibility for our part in it. It means that today we are a little more healthy, sane and serene than we were yesterday. And it means looking at the person in the mirror with love and acceptance rather than judgment and condemnation.

Thank You, God, that I am recovering.

How good it feels to be able to breathe deeply and fill our lungs with fresh air! This simple physical exercise is both a testimony to our growth and a stimulant to our continued healing. Shallow breathing and constricted lungs are too much like our former life of fear and invisibility.

"We are as sick as our secrets" is a slogan often heard in 12-Step recovery circles. It is certainly true for us who kept the secret of incest only to breathe the stale, unhealthy air of abuse and isolation that accompanied it. That dark and dank world no longer has a hold on us.

To be a survivor is to live and to breathe the fresh air of new life.

Thank You, God, for the fresh air of recovery.

Networking begins with contacting a therapist who is also a survivor, subscribing to a survivor newsletter or contacting a 12-Step fellowship for survivors. Once we begin to share with other survivors we find we are not so different or alone after all. Networking opens us to new hope and strength.

Networking breaks the old patterns of isolation and insulation. Now we are tapping our inner strength by connecting with some of the millions of women and men who have survived incest experiences similar to our own. Through networking we find that the energy for surviving — the love for life — is much stronger than the fear and hatred espoused by abusers.

Today I will find strength by reaching out to at least one other survivor.

Friends are people with whom there is mutual sharing, enjoyment and sometimes conflict. In a friendship there is mutual choice-making and limit-setting on how close we are willing to be to each other. These aspects of friendship can be a whole new learning experience for those of us who have come from dysfunctional families with one-sided relationships dominated by our abusers.

Friendship is a two-way street; a friend is someone we have as well as someone we are. Because of similarities in background and some safety structures in 12-Step groups, many of us have developed friendships within our fellowships of recovery. Yet our non-survivor friendships help make life very fulfilling as well. Becoming a good friend to ourself, especially the child within, is a beautiful gift of love.

Thank You, God, for the gift of friendship.

Honesty begins with ourself, particularly as shared with our sponsor, recovery group and Higher Power. Honesty makes no excuses, no rationalizations — just the facts.

Sometimes it may seem brutal, especially if, in being honest, we expose our pain and vulnerability. Secrecy and dishonesty in the past protected our abusers and kept us victims. Being honest with ourselves and with others opens the door to healing.

It can be humiliating to share our shortcomings and deceptions that have adversely affected others. It can also be embarrassing to admit that we have positive and valuable attributes. But honesty accepts both without self-recrimination or applause. We are learning that honesty with self is geared to healing, growth and recovery.

Help me to see myself as I am.

If our minds are closed we can neither learn nor grow, but are doomed to remain in unhealthy patterns of the past. We become our own Higher Power — and thus the judge and jury at whose hands we either condemn ourselves or proclaim our own self-righteousness. We have no need of the group, the Steps, our sponsor or the program. A closed mind quickly restores us to isolation.

Placing principles before personalities is a tested program tradition that encourages us to put our egos aside in order that we might listen to what other recovering incest survivors have found that works. If we remain open-minded, we are in a fertile place open to possibilities for healing and growth.

Help me to keep an open mind.

Lifegiving change only comes with the willingness to say yes. As the Serenity Prayer concludes, "Thy will, not mine be done."

Willingness is one step today. It is trusting in the process of recovery and in the Higher Power who we believe is guiding us through that process. It is more the free-flowing acceptance of a healing grace than a hard-nosed attack on life's problems.

We begin by asking how we can find recovery and come to realize that by being honest with ourselves, having an open mind, and being willing to accept healing, recovery finds us. Recovery is a gift of healing we can prepare ourselves to receive. Incest was devastating. But today we know how to find the way from devastation to new life. And ultimately it is God who grants us the willingness to receive this precious gift.

God, grant me the willingness . . .

Growing up in a family where respect for our boundaries was almost nonexistent is a frequent experience for incest survivors. But now we have the chance to define our boundaries and the right to have them respected.

Initially we may set too rigid boundaries or none at all. We may forget that others have the right to do so for themselves. We are learning. We will make mistakes. But most important is that we are acting on our own behalf.

If we do not have boundaries to define in some sense where we begin and end, how can we invite others into our lives (or say no to those we do not want to come too close)? We deserve to have our space and to have others respect it. Yes, we are a valuable part of a living, breathing universe — but a limited part.

I have the right to set lifegiving personal boundaries.

As children or adults under the domination of a more powerful abuser, we did not have the ability to get away unharmed as our rights were being cruelly violated. Society often reinforced our entrapment.

Even our Higher Power seemed to have abandoned us. We grew into adults and often struggled to gain some control in a world that constantly threatened to overwhelm us. Then we came into program and were told we ought to admit our powerlessness over the incest experience!

In doing so, however, we have come to realize we are powerless over our past — but we need never be helpless again. We know we do not stand alone, but are linked with other survivors in recovery.

I am neither helpless nor alone anymore.

Often as young boys and girls in dysfunctional families we were taking care of adults who could not take care of us.

But this sort of "helping others" only serves to keep us in denial about incest. By focusing on others we avoid dealing with our own pain, hurt, anger, loss, resentment and other recovery issues. We may, in fact, express outward compassion toward others while being harsh on ourselves. We end up intensifying our pain and eventually resenting all those we originally meant to help for "demanding" so much of our time and energy.

It is impossible to feel deeply for another until we have deeply felt our own feelings. Therefore, our most loving service to others begins with a deepening acceptance and compassion toward ourself.

Loving others begins with loving myself.

It is dangerous to mention the night to a survivor for meditation since so many of us associate it with violence, betrayal and secrecy.

It was the abuse that taught us to fear the unknown within ourselves. Yet we, like the summer nights, are filled with warm, comfortable, serene and restful places. We may still be afraid to take a walk outside on warm summer nights, still afraid to enter our dark inner places for fear of what we'll find. But we need no longer believe that only abuse awaits us in the dark.

Summer nights are times to be alone and times to be close with a loved one. Abuse changed aloneness to isolation and closeness to violation. Recovery gives us back the warm summer nights in trust and hope, in inner peace and loving relationship. They are a special place that opens to us as our hearts heal.

Nature embraces me in the warmth of summer nights.

September marks a time of change for many people. Change is especially difficult for incest survivors. We may cope by trying to meet our "new year" with all kinds of resolutions, when what we really need is a deepening trust in our Higher Power.

We may try to control everything, when in truth our very lives are unmanageable. We may want to make others and ourselves "better" so that this time will be different, only to end up after a while giving into old, destructive life patterns and feeling helpless. In other words, we may resolve to redouble our efforts instead of humbly asking for the willingness to let God do for us what we are unable to do for ourselves.

I am not God, but I am of God.

Where before we dreaded life as we knew it, today we are grateful for the blessings and realistic hopes of life beyond incest. Day by day our eyes open to a world filled not with terror and harm, but with promise and hope. Surviving incest through living the 12 Steps leads to a way of life in which serenity and gratitude play a major role.

Gratitude is a form of love in which we are filled with childlike wonder, surprise and enjoyment at our flowing, nurturing relationship with the universe and its Center, our Higher Power. It is especially sweet for incest survivors because we have known such heartache and suffering. At the same time, gratitude is not a "high" or a "pink cloud" experience. It is a stable reality grounded in our daily program of recovery which opens us to the grace of accepting life (and ourselves) on life's terms.

Thank You, God, for the gift of new life through this fellowship.

It doesn't take forever to heal. It might seem like it when, after struggling to disclose or confront, we are met with anger and denial by our abusers and those who support abuse of the innocent.

One day of intense pain can feel like an eternity, but it's only 24 hours (and we don't have to go through it alone). One day of pain gone through in the quest of recovery is another major step in progress and healing. One day of clean, sober, abstinent living is one day of refusing to perpetuate abuse in ourselves or hand it on to others. Recovery doesn't take forever. It only takes one day. Today.

If today is intense, that is because we need to feel intensely today in order to heal. It does get better. Beginning today.

Today is a day of healing and recovery.

When our life becomes filled with busyness, chances are there is little or no room left for ourself. Nothing can be so important that we neglect our physical, emotional and spiritual well-being. Busyness can be the obstacle that prevents us from learning this lesson.

Growing up we often learned to keep moving and stay on the alert. By being busy we simultaneously distracted ourselves from our constant fear of rape while staying inwardly on the alert.

But when we slow down we begin to feel the pain and fear that has been clamoring for our attention all along. Only then can we really feel our feelings and make the choice to let them go. Making room for ourself in our day is a deserving act of self love that helps foster serenity in our lives.

Slow down.

In order to keep surviving, we need to keep opening our hearts in safe places so that we can be filled with the renewing strength of our Higher Power. We know there have been (and continue to be) other victims of incest who haven't made it out alive, whose hearts overburdened, finally gave out.

The best way we can continue to take heart in our recovery and extend that hope to others is by daily nurturing our own hearts. Our hearts are the physical, emotional and spiritual center of our being. There we find en-courage-ment, acceptance, hope and love, for there we are linked with the hearts of all survivors and with the Heart of the universe. Taking time to rest in our own center is to sense our unique value, to know our connection with others and to take heart in the healing process.

Take heart!

When we were being victimized, we knew that an attitude of "let live" toward our abusers only ensured our continued abuse. Today we are able to see this slogan in a different light. We take responsibility for our own lives, including the setting of limits and boundaries. When we are living our own lives with acceptance, love and respect, we are able to let others live theirs without interference. This does *not* mean we ever allow another to perpetrate injustice.

No one has the right to commit crimes against themselves or others. Our silence in the face of this would not be "letting live" but make us silent accomplices. We know the devastation of silence in our own lives: "Live and let live" deepens our respect for life to the point where we become our own best advocates — and advocates for those victims who do not yet have the freedom to live.

Live and let live.

Throughout the ages, many spiritual people have understood their big dreams to be communications from their Higher Power that have led to a deeper understanding of themselves, their relationships with others and of life. Many survivors have big dreams too — some in the form of nightmares, others with feelings of hope and new life. Even our nightmares alert us to the fact that frightening things really happened to us — and that we deserve healing and peace.

It is our right to choose to work with our dreams or not. We may choose to write them down in a journal or share them with a close friend or therapist. But we *never* allow anyone to tell us what our dreams mean if that meaning doesn't feel right to us. Our dreams are a gift of our Higher Power to use as we choose in the healing process.

Dream Maker, teach me what I need to know to heal, to live, to love.

While not all of us came from unhappy homes, many of us felt rejected (or at least not good enough) from the time of our birth. Others of us retreated from life later — after the initiation of incest.

Today we may feel in recovery that real life has finally begun for us. Some of us, however, are still struggling to find out what life is. Wherever we are in the healing process, it is good to remember that because of recovery we are in process — a process of birthing to new life.

Birth — coming to live on our own — is a painful process for mother and child. So it is for us in recovery. We incest survivors are the infants coming to birth. And The Goddess, Nature, God, Higher Power is our true loving and nurturing Mother (and Father) bringing us to new life.

I am coming to new life.

No matter if we have been in recovery a short time or for years, there are times when memories or feelings threaten to overwhelm us. At such times we can feel that all our hard work on recovery may be for naught. We need to remind ourselves: This too shall pass.

During difficult times we can be tempted to turn to former behaviors that used to make us "forget" — addictive substances, caretaking, self-abuse, irresponsibility. We need not indulge but only remember that this too shall pass.

Whether we are feeling high or low, enraged, victimized, exposed, euphoric or whatever else, it will pass as long as we work our program. We will not lose. We will not be violated. We will not be swept away. Recovery is ours and no one can take it away.

This too shall pass.

We survivors know about lighthouses. Our lighthouse is someone who showed us the way when we were confused and could not see, when we needed a friend but were afraid to trust. Such a lighthouse is our hope for new life, someone who cared in our moment of urgent need, our program of recovery. Our lighthouse was the guidance we received out of a life of victimization into one of serenity.

By working the 12 Steps and living the life of recovering incest survivors, we can be lighthouses too — for those out there who are still suffering and for others who are barely surviving. By coming to meetings, using the telephone and being advocates for those who continue to be victimized, we provide the hope of a lighthouse to those out at sea. We are the lighthouse. Higher Power is the beacon. Together we can.

I am a lighthouse.

Prayer and meditation are the means of our daily conscious contact with our Higher Power. Frankly though, for some survivors, even the mention of the word prayer can trigger painful flashbacks. Often it was the very people who abused us who taught us how to pray and who espoused "religious values."

These experiences created for us an image of God who looked an awful lot like our abuser. If we turn to a Higher Power that we believe is abusive in any way, we are still victims. Rather, we need to find a Higher Power that is on our side and to establish daily conscious contact for our healing and growth.

By daily turning to our Higher Power in prayer, we gain an inner strength and guidance for our lives as well as the courage to reach out to other survivors for help when we are in need.

Higher Power, show me the way to new life this day.

Old feelings and thoughts — ghosts of the past — often intrude upon current relationships of incest survivors, leaving us confused.

When feeling confused, we can be helped greatly by calling our sponsor or another trusted program person who has made it through.

When feeling confused and unable to reach another program person, we might try doing a simple task which helps ground us in the present and calms us without blocking out our other feelings entirely. It also gives us a sense of accomplishment in the here-and-now. Or we can monitor our own breathing pattern or heartbeat, just being aware. By focusing our awareness we will naturally center and begin to gain perspective of time and place. Our confusion will pass as feelings come into a more clear, relaxed focus.

Higher Power, be my clarity in times of confusion.

We write primarily for ourselves and for the sake of our healing process.

Writing helps us to express thoughts and feelings that have been locked inside ourselves for years, often beyond our awareness. Our inner monsters become tamed — or at least able to be dealt with — when expressed in the written word.

When our writing first starts to flow it may be filled with all sorts of strong feelings about the incest. In time other expressions will come forth. Because writing is a unique form of expression of who each of us is, it goes far beyond releasing the secrets of our being abused. Through pen and paper the lifeforce within us bears written witness to the worth and beauty of our person.

Higher Power, let the words of truth and liberation come through my hand and pen.

When in the past we fought to survive rather than die, we were saying yes to life. When we continue to live as survivors rather than as victims, we are saying yes to our own lives. When we choose to act in a loving and growth-producing way toward ourselves, we are saying yes to our value and lovableness.

We are so used to saying yes to others (and feeling powerless to say no to them) that we might think we cannot say yes to ourselves. We can and we must in order to grow.

Saying yes is not giving in. Saying yes is not indulging to great excess. Saying yes is loving, caring for and nurturing moderate attitudes and actions directed toward a precious and special person under the guidance of our Higher Power. Each one of us is that special person to whom we are learning to say yes.

Yes, I am worth God's love — and my own!

Hatred is a sign of life because it has so much energy behind it. It can also be an initial antidote to the feelings of apathy and hopelessness that have infected many of us victimized by incest.

Many of us have felt hatred toward ourselves rather than toward the perpetrators. We need to accept the truth of our innocence and affix responsibility where it belongs. While some have always hated and resented our abusers, others are just refocusing onto them the hatred which we used to direct against ourselves. This is a healthy and often necessary healing stage.

In time we may decide to use the energy invested in hating our abusers more profitably for loving ourselves and for reaching out to others who still suffer from victimization.

Higher Power, may my hatred of injustice be in the service of my love for life.

Resentment is what happens to us when our former hatred of the world, our abuser, or ourself becomes frozen through inaction.

Resentment is anger that is "all dressed up with nowhere to go." Resentment is often due to long-held hurt and anger over betrayal and disappointment in an important relationship to which we still cling. Saying goodbye to resentment also means saying goodbye to a fantasy "happy" relationship.

To let go of resentment we need to remind ourself: "To the degree I resent a person, I am emotionally dependent upon that individual." We cannot force another to make restitution willingly for past hurts inflicted upon us. We can ill afford to cling to resentment because it does not change others for the better and only perpetuates self-abuse.

Dear God, heal me of my resentments so that I may let go of self-abuse.

It is *essential* that we externalize the anger we feel for the injustice and betrayal we have endured and express our feelings in non-hurtful ways so that we do not perpetuate violence or abuse. But beneath the angry child is a deeply hurt child filled with loss and grief for the non-existent nurturing parents, innocent childhood and safe world that never was for us in our formative years. And that is a tremendously painful loss to re-experience now in our healing.

If we truly grieve and let them go, we can be empowered to begin a new life of our own. If we do not grieve, the past remains locked within. And what lies ahead is a progression from lonely resentment to constant depression to pervasive numbness. We don't need this anymore.

Higher Power, stay with me in my sadness, grief and tears that seem so deep and unending.

Incest involves the complete denial of grace by perpetrators because (1) they deny the precious beauty of their victims as well as their own and (2) they brutally try to steal satisfaction from a helpless victim rather than looking to a Higher Power for their needs.

Becoming an incest survivor is one of the strongest witnesses to grace in the world because in recovery we attest to the fact that we are beautiful and precious, and we find that God freely gives us what we were unable to achieve on our own. We have only to choose acceptance of this dual gift.

"But for the grace of God . . ." is a slogan frequently heard in 12-Step circles. It is our way of reminding ourselves that through this program so many of us have come into contact with a Higher Power that has saved our lives.

But for the grace of God . . .

Panic attacks (also anxiety attacks) can overwhelm us at times, seemingly out of the blue. From within and without we feel surrounded, under attack and completely defenseless.

We are re-experiencing our feelings from our past when we were unexpectedly betrayed and raped. Our current panic attacks are our body's way of validating our past experience and encouraging us to live through the feelings of that experience so we can let them go.

We need not and should not try to handle panic alone. Multiple resources work best for most of us. A sensitive therapist to help work it through, a caring sponsor we can call when in need, a supportive survivor group where we feel safe — all help us in our transformation from the horror of panic to the strength of serenity.

Be with me through my times of fear and panic.

Work is a double-edged sword for incest survivors. It can be a means of directing our energy
in positive, self-affirming, self-providing ways. It
can also be a means of escaping from ourselves.
The former is a sign of recovery. The latter can
lead to workaholism.

Why do we work? We have to work in order to
support ourselves. We learn in recovery that we
have the right to support ourselves and that we
are capable of doing so. Furthermore, we have
found a Higher Power and a program that supports our recovery.

Our primary work is recovery. Feeling the
support of our Higher Power, our program and
ourselves, we know we do not need to stand in
isolation but are understood by loving others.
From this, all our other work flows. Unlike the
workaholic we do not work to escape life, but to
claim it as our own.

My work is Higher Powered.

Many incest survivors who learned to be care-takers in our youth have grown up to become professional caretakers. Some of us have done this by entering one of the helping professions. Others have devoted our primary energies to homemaking and taking care of others' needs to the neglect of our own.

None of these alternatives has enabled us to have a long lasting sense of personal worth because they all involve something we *do* rather than someone we *are*. Our value, our worth, our specialness comes from who we are. If our worth flows from who we are, then we need to accept and appreciate ourselves. Each of us is a unique and valued person who is part of a lov-ing universe.

Higher Power, walk with me on my journey of coming to accept and celebrate my personal worth.

What is it that we hunger for? Each of us needs to address this question on a daily basis. As children we hungered for unconditional love and to express ourselves without fear of rejection. But instead others used us to feed their own distorted hunger.

Healthy people are aware of hunger and feed themselves with nourishing food. On the contrary, we incest survivors are unaware of our physical, emotional and spiritual hunger except in a way that is all out of proportion. We either gorge on food or fast.

We are learning to listen to our hunger and to give ourselves the food that truly satisfies. We are learning to set limits in responding to our hunger so that we are neither starving nor stuffed. Responding to our hunger means receiving the love, nurturance and acceptance that we have always deserved.

Higher Power, give me the food that truly nourishes.

For us incest survivors the healing process is one more of "discovery" than "recovery."

We may be between 20 and 80 years old and still not know what a healthy life is about. Our healing process, our journey of discovery, is there to help us learn how to live. There is life beyond incest and addiction, beyond hurt and self-destruction — and we need to discover what that means for us.

The distinction is important for those of us who never knew unconditional love and nurturance. We need to understand that when others use the term recovery, it translates for us as discovery. We are learning and discovering for the first time that love, nurturance and healthy living are not only basic to life, but are for us to enjoy.

Every day I am discovering that life can be a blessing for me.

Who are we? Human beings, imperfect. Good and acceptable just because we live and breathe by the grace of a power greater than ourselves.

Where are we? Somewhere along the road of discovery, recovery, healing. Wherever we are right now is a good place to be because our Higher Power is here with us. This loving Higher Power does not want us to be victimized in any way. We are in a process of liberation and new life.

How are we doing? We are healing. At our own pace. In a time frame that our Inner Guide knows is just right for us. Our Higher Power knows we are perfectly acceptable right now in our imperfections. We are okay just as we are.

Who I am, where I am, as I am — today — is good.

The inner voices that seem to have a life of their own inside us tell us we are no good, hateful, ungrateful, lying, seductive persons who deserve to be punished. Perhaps if we punish ourselves, they tease, the Big Person (who looks a lot like our abuser dressed up as "God") might let us live.

All of us have these old tapes that play in our heads and hearts. Many of us find it hard to let them go. Why? Because they are so seductive. They try to make us believe that by acting in a certain (self-destructive) way we can prevent further abuse. They give us the illusion of a little control in a world that feels so out of control. But we know where to find a power greater than our old tapes. It is a Higher Power found in the fellowship of a 12-Step program. Now is the time to begin letting go of self-destructive tapes and trust our healing process.

_____

Higher Power, help me to hear Your voice of love and healing.

There are many who have not survived incest. Some have been killed through the brutality of their attackers. Others have died from a destructive lifestyle activated by abuse. Still others have committed suicide because there seemed no other way to escape the suffering of incest.

The very fact that we are alive today attests to the strength of the life force within us despite all the hatred, manipulation and violence we have endured.

We deserve to live. We deserve to enjoy life. We deserve to become the persons we were meant to be. We have a fellowship of survivors who, like us, have fought the struggle of life and death, and who will support us daily in seeking the life we deserve to live.

I deserve to live life and enjoy life.

When survivors gather, some of us often bring along a friend in the form of a teddy bear, doll or other love object. By hugging and holding our cuddlies we love and nurture ourselves in ways that we really need now — and were often deprived of as children.

What is important here is that we are learning to love ourselves. Having a cuddly is one possible means to that end which some survivors have found helpful.

Cuddlies remind us that whether or not we have natural children of our own, the inner child of our past is still present. Each of us is our own first child. During times when we are quick to criticize or berate ourselves, we might instead treat our inner child with love and respect.

I am a lovable child of God.

Having our innocent trust betrayed when we were so vulnerable makes risking to trust once more a very scary proposition.

Our experience is like that of a person whose apartment was ransacked by a burglar who turned out to be a trusted family member — and who then denied all accusations of wrongdoing. When we gain the self-esteem to protect ourself, we might install all kinds of security locks and alarms. But can we ever risk leaving the door open again?

We can. We begin to find people in our fellowship who understand our suspicions from their own experiences and measure up to our criteria for trusting. In time we become more and more convinced that there might be a Higher Power who loves us unconditionally. The more we experience unconditional acceptance, nurturance and support, the more we become willing to open and trust at a deeper level.

Higher Power, I place my trust in You.

In ancient times to know someone's name was to have a certain power over them as well as a nearness in relationship.

As we survivors learn and grow we begin to value the specialness (sacredness) of our own persons. For some of us the experience of freedom in life is altogether new. It is not unusual to choose a new name that symbolizes our new life and to leave behind the name given in an abusive family. Others do not change names, but begin to value the name and the person it symbolizes with love and reverence.

Choosing our own name means being able to pronounce it and hear ourselves called by name as a blessing rather than a curse. It means accepting life on life's terms. It is a continuing choice of our own destiny in response to the call of a Higher Power.

———————

Dear God, I know You love me because You have called me by name.

A process involves fits and starts, progress and backsliding, good days and bad days. This is true for surviving incest, which is a continuing process of healing and new life. It does not happen overnight, but our experience of life does consistently get better (even though there are times we may actually *feel* worse).

Knowing that our healing journey is a process can frustrate those of us who want instant healing, but it can also support and encourage us who otherwise feel isolated. Recovery from the devastation of incest is a process that always occurs in relationship — our relationship with our fellowship, our Higher Power and ourself.

Finally, it is okay to be the imperfect human beings that we are — always in process, never with it all together. The process of learning to live anew lets go of perfection and makes room for enjoyment.

I am in process.

Sharing is a gift of self to another. In our 12-Step fellowship we share experience, strength and hope with others who know what it means to be survivors of incest. When we choose to share, we are transforming a gap of isolation into a bridge of shared loss and shared hope. We are building communication and community.

When we read survivor literature we are often reading the deeply personal sharing of other survivors with whom we can identify and feel hope. When we either speak or listen at meetings we are part of the giving and receiving process of sharing that is recovery in process.

Sharing is an empowering tool through which we incest survivors find healing and new life. We are learning to choose life through prudent sharing of ourselves.

Teach me to share in life-giving ways.

The process of healing is much more something we are *in* rather than something we can control. Letting go and trusting the process takes courage and risk.

The process of healing and liberation might be scary at times. Explosive anger and rage, tears that never seem to run dry and a feeling that all this is endless might tempt us to distrust what is happening to us. Each of our experiences is unique, but we all share a common heritage of surviving sexual abuse. There is a common ground of having been wounded and a common process in healing.

Trusting the process means trusting the ways in which other survivors have found healing in our 12-Step fellowship and trusting the wisdom of our inner guide (Higher Power). It is the means by which a new life of recovery becomes a reality for us.

Trust the process.

Hugs can be healing, non-invasive forms of touch if given and received with mutual permission and respect.

A child brought up in a loving and accepting environment will spontaneously hug and be hugged, trusting in the goodness of human affection. But one who has known manipulation and betrayal of affection soon becomes confused and hesitant. That child, now an adult survivor, may need a lot of non-tactile love and support before being able to trust a hug again.

When we feel secure about our boundaries and when we can feel that human touch was meant to be supportive, loving and non-invasive, then we can risk hugging. It can be an experience of healing through mutual vulnerability and risk if we are ready for it. If we are not, we might want to try hugging with our cuddly for now.

Higher Power, let it be Your embrace I give and receive in every hug.

When we were victims of incest, it was like being the living dead. We fought with everything we had to maintain some semblance of life, but was being an incest victim living?

The path of recovery turns all that around by giving us the promise of new life. At times that can be scary. (Will we make it through?) But being with other survivors who are just as determined to make it fills us with hope.

Our passage is truly one of death to life, betrayal to trust, isolation to intimacy. We have to be willing to do the footwork trusting that our Higher Power will supply the grace. Yes, our abusers may have instilled in us the belief that a living death was all we deserved, but we know better than that now. We are willing to do whatever it takes to make it through.

The only way out is through.

What can be helpful in the healing process? Actually, anything that we enjoy, that demonstrates self-nurturance, and in which we are open to healing. A hot bath is one specific example.

As victims our right to privacy was not respected; now we claim that right. As victims our abusers often demanded we be at their beck and call; now we take as much time as we choose to care for our own needs. As victims, another's gentleness or kindness was often coupled with a demand for sex. Now we can soak in soothing love without anyone demanding we pay up.

Something as simple as a hot bath can be a sacred ritual, a healing sacrament. We are soaking in the warmth and cleansing and relaxation that we deserve. In such a simple act as this we are renewing our spirit.

Today God's love is a nice hot bath.

Living as a survivor rather than as a victim means having the willingness to keep on working our program to the best of our ability, in union with our Higher Power. There are plenty of temptations to do otherwise. We are newcomers to program and the feelings that are coming up threaten to overwhelm us. Or we have been around program for a while and figure we should be all better by now. Maybe the routine of the program begins to bore us.

There are plenty of reasons for abandoning our program of healing and recovery. When they begin to draw us away from our 12-Step way of life, however, we may need to remind ourselves to keep on keeping on. The program that has saved us from a lifetime of victimization offers us a guarantee of continued serenity and survival — if we are willing to work it.

Keep on keeping on.

Newcomers are the autumn trees of 12-Step fellowship. Their tears, struggle, confusion and risk attract our attention and wonder like no other. They remind us of the depth of our pain and of our continuing dying process (dying to the role of victim) so that we might live more fully as survivors. Their presence, like the autumn leaves, points not only to winter but to the hope of spring and summer to follow.

In a sense all of us are newcomers. All of us risk time and again our pain and struggle that call attention to the crime of incest so that we and others might find new life. In doing so we validate the truth of each others' lives as well as our own. We continue in the process that has its moments of brilliance, awe and wonder in the midst of our healing pain.

Higher Power, be with us through our seasons of healing.

Many child abuse survivors have gaps in child-hood memories. Some can only remember the good times. Some of us only feel unattached fear or self-hatred. In these instances we are suffering from amnesia.

There are, of course, survivors who seem to remember every last detail of the abuse. How-ever, many of us have forgotten. Our minds just blocked out such a traumatic betrayal of trust. Amnesia was for us a survival mechanism.

Because our abusers and family members called us liars, we tend to doubt our own memo-ries when they now return. But they will return when we are ready to accept them. Our memo-ries come not only in mental words and pictures, but in smells, sounds, sensations, feelings and bodily distress. We can more readily heal when we welcome and accept our memories, no matter how distressing they may be.

Higher Power, help me to believe the truth of my memories.

Touch is meant to heal, to love, to connect, to create, to affirm, to bless, to value. How strange this sounds to us who were victimized by the violent touch of incest! But it is true. Our abusers distorted and misused touch as a means of satisfying their own needs — and in the process betrayed us.

As survivors today we are empowered to say, "No, you cannot touch me," and "Yes, you may touch me in such a way under these circumstances." We thus reclaim ownership of our personal boundaries and begin to experience touch when we feel ready and with persons who feel safe to us. We begin to learn of the gentle gift touch was always meant to be.

Touch is our physical connection with the universe. What was formerly used to betray us is now the healing touch befriending us and reconnecting us with a loving world.

Higher Power, let me feel Your healing touch today.

We have risked everything we have ever known in the hope of discovering a new world. We are adventurers from a world of victimization in search of serene survival. We have lived in isolation too long and are now risking lifegiving fellowship.

The 12 Steps are the map we are following. The journey, we know, has its struggles as well as joys, but the many who have gone before us encourage us along the way. No matter how long the road seems, "one day at a time" and "easy does it" is the sound advice we follow.

Old tapes of victimization are the heritage our abusers gave us to carry into our adult years. But a new world of hope and discovery is the promise of 12-Step fellowship. We are learning to say no to the old tapes and a resounding yes to this new world.

I choose to live in a new world of love and hope.

We incest survivors have usually been persons of extremes regarding the expression of anger. Some of us, embittered by our past, have gone through life with a giant chip on our shoulders. Many others have buried or masked our anger, always trying to be nice, good, helpful.

As victims we were given the message that we had no right to our anger, that we deserved the abuse. No matter how much this confused us, we have always known deep down that our anger was justified. And now as survivors we are learning healthy, productive, non-violent expressions of our anger in the face of past and present injustices.

Because we revere ourself and all living beings, anger is now our spontaneous response to abuse.

Healing anger is my path to healing love.

Peace is a gift of our Higher Power like no other. More than calm, peace is serenity. More than freedom from external conflict, peace is a safe and secure harbor at the center of our being. More than a word or a wish, peace is a new and gentle way of life.

None of us can manufacture peace, but we can do the footwork to help open our heart to receive this healing gift. Since a Higher Power is the source of peace, we need to remove the obstacles that keep us stuck in a life of isolation and victimization. And we need to connect with other survivors in recovery who, like us, are willing to commit to a 12-Step way of life.

Such a continued commitment on our part involves risk against our fear and anxiety. Those who have taken such risks are reaping the blessings of peace.

Higher Power, be my peace.

Meetings are gatherings of two or more people who come together to share experience, strength and hope as survivors of incest.

Many of us when left all alone — no matter how long we have been in recovery — tend to deny and invalidate our experiences of the past (both our wounds and our healing). Meetings reinforce our memories of the past and our growing positive feelings about ourselves. They help us learn to relate safely with persons of both sexes. They provide a means of advocacy toward those who are still victims of incest or its effects.

Meetings guarantee us a place to go when we might otherwise be victimizing ourselves in various ways. They are also an opportunity for service (not unhealthy caretaking) where we give witness to the healing process by our commitment to this program.

I commit myself to attend the next available survivor meeting.

Fusion and confusion are two words that go together for incest survivors. When we did not yet have a developed sense of ourselves and our feelings, older, more powerful persons caused us great damage by imposing their emotional needs on us.

So, many of us grew up confused. We went to great lengths to defend our abusers (especially if they were our parents) as if we were defending ourselves. Our own identities had become fused with theirs.

Our healing process leads us to the realization that we deserve and can have a genuinely happy life of our own. We are not responsible for the well-being of our abuser. We need to discover our own feelings and appreciate our unique self. In order to do this we must day by day let go of the unhealthy bond that fused us emotionally with the perpetrator. Only then will we be free.

I do not need abuse or abusers.

Sadness is an ordinary part of life. It is not all there is to life, but it is a very real part. No one lives a perfect childhood. Everyone endures some wounds and losses.

It is okay to feel our sadness. We may cry a lot. We may become angry or depressed as well as sad. But sadness itself will not destroy us or anyone else.

Most of us grew up in places where it was not safe to be vulnerable, to feel our sadness, to cry. Today we have safe places to feel, whether they are in our groups, with a trusted friend or therapist or alone with our Higher Power. When we allow ourselves to begin re-experiencing a lifetime worth of sadness bit by bit, we begin to heal. We begin to move to a point where sadness and incest does not occupy us 24 hours a day. We begin to find hope in life beyond incest, beyond our deep sadness.

It is okay to be sad.

As physical beings, sexuality and sensuality are the ways in which we relate with a physical universe. Yet these are the aspects of our lives that are so deeply wounded. Our sexuality was beautiful, innocent and spontaneous — until we were cruelly taken advantage of.

Some of us grew to hate and fear our sexuality because we were told our beauty was irresistible and we thus "asked" for the rape. At times we overvalued the power of our sexuality and came to hate sexual desire in ourself and others. Some of us turned cold to any sexual feelings or became sickened by arousal.

Many of us, however, are reclaiming a healthy sexuality. We are learning to appreciate the beauty of being a responsible sexual person. We feel a tremendous boost in self-esteem in defining the limits of our relating as sexual beings.

I am a beautiful sexual being.

It can be disheartening after a long time of working our program to feel as though we have got no better. The old fears and anxieties may return, self-destructive behavior may reactivate and hopelessness may begin to dominate our feelings. At such times it is important to remember that setbacks are temporary; recovery is for life.

Setbacks are only temporary if we are willing to keep on living the Steps and using the tools of recovery. Setbacks often precede a stage of new growth. In this way they can be viewed as signs of renewed hope rather than hopelessness.

Even though an abuser in the present (or abusive behaviors internalized as a result of our past) may threaten our stability, we are no longer helpless victims but empowered survivors.

Higher Power, lead me to new growth beyond my setbacks.

Compassion is a very deep and special form of love. In compassion, a person's heart is wide open and thus very vulnerable.

Many of us incest survivors began at an early age to practice compassionate caring for others. We were not afraid to be with others in their suffering. Yet most of us never learned to be compassionate with ourselves.

The healing process invites us to receive compassionate caring from those who know and understand our suffering — usually other survivors in recovery. This process also teaches us how to be compassionate and understanding with ourselves, no matter what. Compassion teaches us an unconditionally accepting love, free of criticism toward a beautiful yet wounded person — ourself.

Dear God, heal me with Your compassionate love.

To value, to honor, to respect — these are the gifts we give when we esteem someone. Have we not been stingy in offering these gifts to ourself? Most probably the answer has been yes.

Abuse lied to us, told us we were worthless, robbed us of esteem. Healing and recovery offer us the opportunity to accept the gift of self, maybe for the very first time. We are learning to esteem ourselves.

God (or however we understand our Higher Power) is the ultimate source of this gift. We exist because we were thought to be highly respectable, valuable, honorable. We were loved into existence. Though we have been abused, the gift of a growing self-esteem reminds us of the priceless gift each of us is.

I am the honor of God.

For many incest victims, faith has meant belief in a distant God and a no-good self. Such a faith only perpetuated our victimization. If we were fortunate, we were able to let go of such beliefs. But where did that leave us? Often alone and unhappy.

When we came into program, we were told we needed to believe in a Higher Power. The Higher Power of our abusers betrayed us. The Higher Power of religion seemed to have abandoned us. And now we were being told that in order to heal we needed to have faith in a Higher Power! Difficult as it was to believe this, many of us successfully risked putting our faith in a loving Higher Power.

We believe there is a Higher Power that is on our side — the side of survival, life and love — and who is never abusive. This kind of faith has saved us for life.

I believe in a Higher Power who loves me unconditionally.

The emptiness we have felt, and sometimes still feel, can seem overwhelming. We have been so under-loved and abusively "loved" that there never seems there could be enough of the real thing.

These feelings can be misleading. They can lead us to consume increasingly greater amounts of sugar, alcohol, narcotics, caffeine and nicotine in our attempt to fill the bottomless pit. Or they can lead us from one bad relationship to another, looking for the ideal lover and friend. They can lead us to isolation and alienation.

The feeling of a bottomless pit is, however, a positive signal of our need for healing and recovery. It is telling us we have a legitimate right to be loved for our own sake and not for another's abusive gain. The 12-Step path of healing shows us the lifegiving way to have these deep needs met.

God, You are my enough.

When we do not trust our memories we feel as if we are about to go over the edge into complete insanity.

Often behind our feelings of being crazy is amnesia blocking out the painful memories of our abuse. We who remember the abuse may minimize the debilitating influence it has had on our lives. Unwittingly, we come to believe the insanity is ours rather than that of incest.

We do not have to let our abuse drive us to insanity or suicide. We might instead accept the reality of our value in the eyes of our Higher Power and the reality of our betrayal by another for selfish gain. The question we eventually come to face honestly is: What does it mean for me that I was once (or many times) betrayed by a trusted other and am now a survivor of incest?

Insanity is not to believe in my worth.

We cannot do it all. We cannot achieve full recovery from incest all at once, so we only do what we can for today. We cannot save all victims of incest, but we can begin carrying the message to at least one other person.

Doing more is not the answer; setting limits is.

When we set limits we mark off our boundaries and thus establish a place that is safe and secure — whether or not others approve. When we set limits we discover that saying yes to ourselves might sometimes mean saying no to others. Setting limits marks the ownership of the personal space and identity we need. Only by setting limits do we have a personal space into which we may choose to invite another and from which we can continue to grow.

Thank God I know my limits.

Advocacy is speaking out on behalf of someone in need, especially people who do not have a powerful voice of their own. If anyone in our society is disempowered it is our children. Because children are by nature dependent and receptive, they need advocates who reverence their innocence, trust and fragility.

Every survivor is one of those children. We might be grown-ups on the outside, but on the inside lives an innocent, lovable, needy, wounded, betrayed child. A major part of the healing process for each of us is to learn how to become a responsible advocate for that child.

In order to heal and to flourish, children need a safe place. And they need love — spontaneous, genuine, deeply felt, without strings attached. We are those children. We can be those advocates too.

I am a loving advocate for my inner child.

Who is that setting new world speed records for hyperactivity? Is it one of us survivors (or many of us) racing around from one activity to the next? Why are we so afraid to slow down?

It is not unusual for us survivors to become so busy that we cannot feel ourselves in the present. "There is too much to be done," is our excuse. Feeling our feelings in the here-and-now can be quite intimidating. We cannot control what will surface next from within — unless we move too fast to feel.

Slow down. It's okay to feel whatever we feel. We will not disintegrate. In a peaceful place — a safe place — we can listen to our feelings; we can share; we can know we are loved. Slow down . . .

In a quiet place I become aware of my feelings and embrace myself in love.

The more we begin to accept our feelings and memories that validate our experiences, the more we may feel, for a time, that we are completely out of control. This feeling can be misleading. In fact, flashbacks and other reminders of the abuse only come when we have reached a relatively safe place in our lives where we can begin to deal with the reality of incest.

When we feel safe and free to be ourselves we have no compulsive need for control. Our abusers in their insecurities used manipulation, power and domination to control us. We can turn away from their unhealthy example by choosing to live in a safe universe and associating with people who encourage openness and the freedom to be oneself without the use of violence.

I can let go of the need to control because I feel safe to be me.

Victims see repulsiveness and disgust in the mirror; survivors see strength and beauty. Victims see everything that is wrong and imperfect; survivors see a reflection of the image of God. Victims see a picture of despair; survivors gaze upon an image of hope. Victims often see an unlikable adversary; survivors see an innocent child.

Looking into the mirror of our bodies, our feelings and our souls can be very difficult for a while because we might begin by seeing ourselves through our abusers' rejecting eyes. But the more honestly we look into the mirror, the more our sight clears and becomes our own. Survivor meetings can be helpful places for looking into the mirror of ourselves as reflected among kindred spirits — our fellow survivors.

I see beauty, strength and lovableness as a reflection of my true nature.

Most of us grew up believing that in order to safeguard our integrity we had to wall ourselves off from others and rely only on ourselves. We carried this attitude into our sexual relationships as well. Either we had nothing to do with sex or engaged in it indiscriminately. We had no model for healthy sexual relationships.

Deep within we might long for love but throw our bodies around as though we are worthless. One of the definitions of promiscuous is "confused." This fits us to a tee. In the most physically intimate situations we could not have been more isolated.

Healing from incest means reclaiming our feelings and letting go of indiscriminate and confused behavior in favor of stable, lifegiving relationships.

I deserve healthy relationships.

How many of us cringe at the mere mention of the word "forgiveness!" How many of us are filled with guilt or anger at hearing others question, "Why don't you just forgive and forget?" Yet forgiveness is not such a simple matter for incest survivors. We need only forgive ourselves.

Besides, we cannot forgive others unless we truly love and forgive ourselves. If we love ourselves freely, then we can hold no grudges about our past behaviors, feeling we should have somehow acted other than the ways in which we did. Forgiveness of others takes time. After we have bathed deeply in love, we come to see that hanging onto bitter resentments is just another form of self-hatred and unhealthy dependency. Only when we really *feel* and *believe* this are we ready to move onto forgiveness of others. And then we recognize that it is a lifegiving gift to ourself as well.

I forgive myself; I lovingly accept my human limitations.

Relationships (abusive) betrayed and hurt us; relationships (healing) will bring us new life and serenity. Perhaps all we knew growing up were abusive relationships. These resulted in wounds, brokenness and isolation. Such relationships were governed by fear, domination and control. They are always one-sided and destructive.

Healing relationships, on the contrary, teach us that our true nature is not apart from one another (separatist), but a part of one another (in communion).

As we learn to love deeply and respect ourselves, we grow in reverence for all creation. No person, no part of the universe, is ours to dominate or manipulate. Each is potentially a means of healing relationships.

I am a valuable part of all that is.

Every night was trick or treat for children who grew up in dysfunctional homes. We put on our best faces and opened our arms in trust to the big people we so needed. Sadly there was often a cruel trick under the wrappers of the treats they offered us. "Don't take candy from strangers," they warned. But what about it when the cruel trickster offering candy was Mom or Dad?

Most of our homes put on nice faces for neighbors, church and school. For us these were confusing disguises that turned almost every promising treat into a mean trick. We have longed for the treat without the trick. However, it is a mistake to keep on looking for it from such a fantasy family. Our true family is found in the healing relationships we are building today with those who love and accept us without trickery.

Thank You, God, for the love and support of dear friends.

What do incest survivors look like? Hysterical women? Child-molesting men? People too tainted, too screwed-up for normal society? These are the stereotypes. They are not true.

Incest survivors come from all walks of life. There are a superabundance of us in the helping professions — but this does not define us either.

As victims our fear often was, "Everyone can see how worthless, tainted, dirty I am." As survivors we begin to see and love the beauty of our true nature, and we discover that the ugliness was in the crime committed against us. What do we look like? On the outside we look like any other adult. Come closer and see that we are women and men who have known deep suffering and who possess a deeper love for life.

I am a beautiful person.

Not everyone is gifted in expressing feelings, memories and experiences in words. Some communicate best in non-verbal images, sounds or body movement. Because many of us experienced hurt or rejection before we could speak, our memories often best come out in these non-verbal ways.

Art involves drawing, painting, sculpting, modelling — anything that translates experience into image. We do not have to be good at it or to be trained in order to express ourselves through art. All we have to do is take a paper and crayons and let the feelings flow.

Art is therapeutic for incest survivors because it enables us to give shape and form to our feelings and see them outside ourselves. Abuse is not the totality of our experience of self. Artistic expression helps to bring that realization home.

I am breaking secrets through my art.

Music has a way of tapping into memories and feelings that we otherwise might not have ready access to. Hearing a piece of music can put us directly in touch with feelings and experiences that might be lost to us otherwise.

The value of this type of experience is not to perpetuate feelings of sadness or sentimentality, but to connect them with their cause, to re-experience them as validating our past, and to let them go as part of our healing process. Music can be a powerful reconnecting force because it goes beyond left-brain logic to include right-brain experience.

Playing a musical instrument and singing are expressive, healing modalities in which some of us engage. Both serve not only as a cathartic release of our pent-up feelings, but as creative expressions of who we are.

The music of my soul praises the Divine in the human.

To move, to dance, to express oneself through the spontaneous feeling and movement of self as body — how threatening, how freeing! And how impossible and remote it seems for those of us whose bodies meet the world hunched over and protected or frozen stiff. But in truth, freeing dance begins with the simplest movements.

It is okay to move as our trapped inner child desires. It might be crawling around on the floor in the safety of one's own room. Or stretching exercises might be all we can manage at first. We are feeling and moving in our bodies for the sake of our lives.

Body movement and dance set free the imprisoned child. The hurt and anger, the love and grace, everything that identifies our "me-ness" comes out in its beauty and starkness. Dance overcomes the silence and lies of incest.

I might feel awkward, but I am dancing for my life!

People can have a way of pushing our buttons and stirring our feelings of guilt if we are used to giving to others without caring for ourselves. By refusing to let guilt and fear rule us, we are setting boundaries which say, "This I will do and no more" and "I will not indulge in that which harms my body and spirit." Saying yes begins by learning to say no to that which separates us from ourselves.

We realize that what formerly appeared to be acts of kindness were actually acts of self-abuse. By saying no to them we reverence ourselves as persons. We cannot freely love and care for anyone else unless we first accept and respect ourself — who we are, how we feel and what we want in life.

Yes begins with No.

Every day is a new opportunity to recommit ourselves to our healing and growth. At times we can get tired of going to meetings or identifying ourselves as incest survivors. But to be in the healing process means to move away from a self closely linked to incest to one of survivor and thriver in life.

Our childhoods were devastated by incest. Life was lived in a constant state of hyper-alertness for the next attack.

Recommitting our lives to ourself means letting go of the hypervigilance about what someone else might do or feel, and paying attention to how we feel and what we really want to do. Old self-destructive patterns can't creep back if we recommit to loving and caring for ourselves one day at a time.

I dedicate this day to my healing and growth.

Healing from incest and living a new life takes place one day at a time. Upon realizing we are incest survivors, we might want to work through this problem and be done with it once and for all. Or we might feel overwhelmed at the pervasive effects of incest in our lives and wonder if recovery will take forever.

Recovery from the effects of incest does not take forever, but healing is a way of life which takes place one day at a time. Recovery is a process of learning to live a healthy, abuse-free life.

We need the courage just for today to let go of our self-abuse and of associating with people who abuse us. When we start putting those 24-hour periods back-to-back we begin to realize the joy of love and of life that can fill the emptiness once occupied by abuse.

One day at a time.

As adult survivors of childhood sexual abuse we have a choice. We can deny that anything ever happened to us and continue to live a fantasy life, we can admit we are survivors but still cling to the victim role or we can choose to do whatever it takes to achieve healing and growth.

While we might move in and out of denial regarding the reality of the abuse, the fact that we would even read such a book as this or be involved in a 12-Step program indicates that we are unwilling to remain in denial. The real struggle for many of us is admitting we are survivors while still clinging to the victim role and self-abusive life patterns. We need to remember to be gentle with ourselves because such behaviors are deeply ingrained and discarded only with great difficulty. The choice is ours alone to make.

We have a choice.

Loss means change. A relationship, a hope, a way of life we once had (or thought we had) is no longer there for us. Grieving, crying, mourning, raging are the healthy and natural ways to process loss. Shock and denial sometimes precede these when our loss feels overwhelming.

For survivors, loss often meant betrayal by a very important person in our lives. Some of us became stuck in chronic shock and stubborn denial for years. A feeling can persist that acknowledging the loss will destroy us. It will not.

We might cry and rage, feel deeply hurt, betrayed and rejected, even feel that our whole world has been turned upside down. However, the grieving process and its accompanying feelings are signs of life, not death. Loss hurts — yes. But it opens us to a life of possibilities.

The pain of loss is a passageway; denial is a locked door.

Each of us is a part of nature — a necessary and valuable part. We are not the hateful persons we used to see in the mirror. We are not the worthless creatures our abusers would have us believe. We are born of nature and sustained by nature. We are of value.

The earth is our true and lasting Mother. She gave us birth. She feeds us. And she sustains us. All through our lives there is not one moment when Mother Earth is not supporting us in every step of life's journey.

The air that we breathe, the atmosphere in which we live is our life-preserving Father. He is always there for us, allowing us to take whatever we need. These parents sustain us; they will never betray us. Nature is our true home.

I am a valuable part of nature.

Tears are not suffering or pain. Nor are they anger or rage. Tears are not joy or gratefulness. No, tears are a release, a letting go, an externalizing of that which is within us. Letting go is another phrase for grieving or mourning.

Some of us were so hurt, angered and confused by the abuse we suffered that our tears became frozen within. We may have sworn we would never cry again or we simply could not cry no matter how much it burned inside. Tears seemed a sure sign of vulnerability.

Many of us whose tears were long frozen can cry daily for weeks or months when the tears start to flow. Tears can overcome us anywhere, but generally they come when we begin to feel safe — safe within ourselves, with trusted friends and in our surroundings.

Dear God, grant me the grace of letting go.

We are gifted, every one of us. After what we have been through, it is not only a gift but a major miracle that we are even alive today to tell our stories.

Some of us might find ourselves squirming in our seats or saying "that's crazy" to any suggestions that we might be gifted persons. But it is far from crazy. What was crazy was for our abusers to act as though we were not precious gifts of the Divine, deserving love and respect. That was insane.

Our existence is a gift. Our vulnerability is a gift. Our strength is a gift. Gifts can be misused and abused — we know that. That is how some others responded to the gift in us. But that is not our response. We are survivors. We are thrivers. We live to cherish the unique gift of the universe that is our very self.

I cherish the gift of my person.

Enthusiasm literally means to be filled with the gods, the Divine — whatever that means to us. And yet that seems completely impossible to the incest victim who knows only unspeakable emptiness.

How do we get from desolation to enthusiasm? It might help to realize that before any perpetrators brought us to the pit of empty desolation, our true nature was open to the fullness of the wonders of creation.

Where does the enthusiasm come from? Not from our family of origin parents, not from the perpetrators of our abusive past. It comes from the loving universe which called us into being. Life takes on enthusiasm the more we let go of the victim role and begin to live as survivors and thrivers.

I will give no one the power to make me forget that my heart is filled with enthusiasm.

There are millions of dependent children and adults who continue to be victimized by incest. And the very best way we can work to change their fate is by dedicating ourselves to our own healing. Only if we make our personal healing the priority in our lives will we be able to carry a message of hope to others.

When we attend meetings and make phone calls to other survivors as part of our healing process, we are also carrying the message to others that we have hope in a new life no matter how rough things can sometimes get. We share recovery by working for it ourselves.

Carrying the message is not focusing on others' pain to avoid our own. It is the direct result of our having had a spiritual awakening by means of living the 12 Steps.

I have a message of hope and of new life to share.

Disclosing is always necessary in the process of healing from childhood sexual abuse.

Disclosing can begin by sharing the fact of being an incest survivor with a therapist, close friend or fellow survivor. Because so many of us doubt the reality of our experience (our abusers often told us nothing happened!), we need to disclose many times and in various circumstances. The more we speak the truth, the more we are heard and validated, the more we believe it ourselves.

Disclosing is making public what ought never to have been held in secret. Disclosing means standing up and saying no one has the right to abuse children. Disclosing validates our pain, yes, but also the force for life and growth within us that is more strong. Disclosing is empowering.

Incest is one secret I choose not to keep.

Confronting the abuser is part of our individual healing process *only if we decide we need it.* Just as disclosing can take various forms of expression, so can confronting. Survivors have confronted their abusers face-to-face, through letter writing, at their cemetery graves, even in the public media. In other words, we have learned to do whatever it takes to validate our experience, whether or not our abusers continue to respond with denial.

Confronting can be a very powerful way to tell our abusers and co-abusers that we are taking responsibility for our own lives — and not for any of their acts of manipulation or violence. It can be a powerful step in defusing, especially where we have taken on our abusers' feelings, guilt and responsibility as our own. Confronting means bringing the truth before the eyes of our abusers, co-abusers and ourselves.

Show me Your ways of truth.

There is no taboo against incest. It happens all the time, to all kinds of people, in all kinds of circumstances. What is taboo about incest? *Telling* is. The oppressive people who support incest are the very ones who made talking about it taboo. And that taboo has been around for thousands of years.

When we were victimized by incest, we lost our voices. Somehow we believed that if we ever told the truth, terrible things would happen. That's how strong the taboo is! That taboo kept us as victims rather than survivors.

But we are not in the victim role anymore. We are choosing healing by choosing to accept the truth, to talk about the truth and to live our lives by the truth. Lies suffocated us; the truth sets us free.

Incest isn't taboo; talking about it is. But I have found my voice. I can talk!

There is a spontaneous letting go, a being and trusting in the universe in play. Children play a lot. Children come into this world innocent and trusting and playful. Play isn't something that a child needs to be taught; a child plays naturally.

At one time we all played. But there came a day when someone we trusted betrayed our trust and manipulated our desire to play into something very overwhelming and scary. We were the victims of a "power play" that had nothing to do with spontaneous fun.

Reclaiming our lives as adults involves freeing the playful child within. Play involves our spontaneous enjoyment of self in relation to the universe. There is no one up or one down in play — just the fun of being alive and enjoying ourselves in relationship.

I am alive — I can play!

An expression of uncontrollable hurt and anger is one description of rage. Rage is a violent reaction to wholesale betrayal — that implodes or explodes.

Rage isn't simple anger at an unjust act; it is the natural response to cruelty, callousness and disrespect for the sacredness of life — especially innocent life. Many of us have bottled up our rage for fear we will kill someone. In fact, it is an energy for life (not death) that just needs some focusing.

Getting some professional guidance on expressing our rage in healthy ways can really help. Being accepted by another during the times we need to rage can be affirming and validating. Our rage ought never be used to destroy our own life or anyone else's but only to free our imprisoned inner children in order to live life anew.

The rage of the abused is a call to life.

Fear of sexuality and of intimate relationships are major issues in our lives.

Whether we try to hide behind layers of clothes, a chunky body or an unfriendly disposition, we cannot deny that our fear of rape is still very much with us. But it is important to remember: We were not raped because we were too attractive or seductive or friendly, but because other persons chose to commit violent crimes.

Sex is scary when we remember that it was used as a means of violence and humiliation against us. Sex is scary when we have not known it as an expresssion of love without manipulation. We can heal. We can love our sexuality. But it takes time, patience, gentleness, understanding and love.

Be patient with me. Beautiful creations are fragile and, when wounded, take time to heal.

Say it with flowers. Tell a loved one how precious they are with a bouquet. You, yourself, are that loved one.

Flowers — the beauty of life in full bloom — or plants — life to be nurtured and cared for — can be reminders of valuable qualities within us. No, we cannot go back to receive the affirmation of our beauty and the nurturance that we did not get the first time around. But we can love and cherish the child who is still within us and the adult we have become.

Why not do something special for that beautiful woman or man victimized by incest? Why not present her or him with a rose or a handful of daisies that says, "I love you"? Why not remember the reason for looking at all this dark and yucky stuff called incest in the first place?

I am beginning to blossom.

We cannot accomplish healing on our own. Because we came from a dysfunctional family background, we have no childhood experience of what healthy is. So what would we aim for? Besides, we need a healing power that is something more than ourself against the world.

Some survivors call this healing force God, Nature, The Goddess, Inner Voice, Higher Power, Deeper Reality, Truth, Recovery Program, etc. Whatever it is, it cannot be just ourself (that is how we have remained victims) or only one specific person (our abuser was one such higher power).

The more we associate with survivors in recovery — and get down on our knees every morning and night — the more we will discover who this Higher Power is for us. It is our source of healing and strength.

Higher Power, let me know that You are here and that You care.

Giving thanks is not about family members who are really isolated from each other, all sitting around a turkey pretending to be happy. Thanksgiving is how we feel when we are able to breathe freely without fear of attack; when we are able to share who we really are — safely — with another person; when we can love without having that love turned on us as a sexual weapon.

Many of us came from families in which we pretended to be happy and were often told to be thankful for our lot in life. That is the kind of thanksgiving that breeds cynicism and despair. We now know there are other reasons to give thanks for: a Higher Power who cares, a universe in which we are a valuable part, a self who is truly lovable. We give thanks that where once was despair now lives hope — in our hearts.

We give thanks for new hope.

Physically and emotionally separating from a dysfunctional family system can be a very difficult task.

We spend time with our former abusers out of family obligation or in the hope they will change. Often it is time spent numbing out or spacing out so as to shield ourselves from continued negativity and put-downs or the very-much-alive ghosts of the past.

It is important to remember we have a choice. By physically and emotionally separating from those who abused us or silently stood by, we can make choices from our own feelings, desires and beliefs, no longer fused with the unhealthy needs of our abusers. Separating can lead to the fearfulness of standing alone. It can also lead to the realization of our inner strength as well as our freedom to choose with whom we want to be close.

God, help me to separate from the lies so that I may come to know the truth.

As children most of us learned to turn off our feelings, to numb, to space out. As we grew up we often turned to some substance (alcohol, drugs, sugar) or activity (spending, gambling, working, caretaking, exercising) that would help us turn away from those bodily signals we call feelings.

Many of us became addicted as it took more and more of the substance or activity to achieve less and less of an effect. We entered a nowhere-land where we could neither safely feel our feelings nor comfortably escape them.

In the safe company of other survivors we can begin to risk feeling and sharing our feelings. They might lead us to express tears, anger, rage, hurt and sadness. But feelings will not destroy us, they only free us to live life.

Be with me in my fear and desire to feel once again.

Perseverance is a very strong trait in incest survivors. We have been through hell in order to survive.

Incest survivors are often people who as adults "can take a lot." The strength of this is that we can make it through hard times; the weakness is that we might let ourselves suffer various forms of abuse in getting through. Since our healing process is quite challenging, we can use our strength of perseverance as a healing tool.

We persevere through long spells of crying, intermittent outbursts of rage and days we feel we have gone nowhere. We persevere in getting to know an inner child who continually tests the notion that anyone could possibly be trustworthy. We persevere in hope, not always "taking it," but making it to a place where we can begin to enjoy ourselves as we are and as we are becoming.

Grant me the grace of perseverance.

Some call it Post-Traumatic Stress Disorder. Others call it "chronic shock." We often think of war veterans and concentration camp survivors as its victims. But we who were children in an unpredictable and threatening living situation often suffer from this, too.

Nightmares, flashbacks and panic attacks are some of its effects. Psychic, emotional numbing in order to survive is another. We split into multiple personalities at times or cannot connect our mental thoughts with our bodily feelings.

We cannot be boxed away with some psychiatric label. By coming together in groups of fellow survivors, we can learn and share and grow. We can realize it is okay and normal for us to want to shut the whole world off at times. We can also discover what is helpful in reconnecting when we are ready.

I have survived the war of abuse and am discovering a new peace.

Fear of paralysis is the paralysis that most commonly afflicts sexual abuse survivors.

We can freeze up today when we are backed into a corner, caught up against a wall or hit with a certain sight, smell, taste, sound or feeling. Any number of triggers can put us back into the paralyzed child. However, we need not knowingly put ourselves into these situations (like going back to the scene of the crime to visit family) if we choose not to.

When thrown unaware into a fearful paralysis, it is important to remember that we have the power to avoid abuse now. We need to be gentle with ourselves and accept our fear and temporary paralysis. But we also need to remember to breathe slowly and deeply, feeling our groundedness and our strength. "This too shall pass."

———

God, be my calm and strength in my times of paralysis.

Sometimes thirst can be very threatening to us who are sexual abuse survivors. The awareness of our neediness and incompleteness reminds us of our vulnerability, our need to go outside ourselves to have our inner needs filled. The other side of that fear, however, is the realization that we can choose what is healthy and lifegiving to slake our thirst.

We physically thirst for water; we need not fill it with alcohol which numbs and kills, but with water, juices and milk which nourish. We emotionally thirst for love and intimacy; we need not fill it with abusive relationships, but with persons with whom we can share mutual love and care. We spiritually thirst for union with God; we need not make any person, place or thing our God, but find the God within who is really the source of our creativity, love and life.

I thirst for You, O God.

H.A.L.T. is a lifegiving measure to preserve us from self-destruction when we may not even realize that we are having feelings. It is an acronym that stands for *H*urt, *A*ngry, *L*onely, *T*ired. The name also suggests what we need to do — halt or stop in our tracks — before we cause harm to ourselves or others.

We can still carry around our old abusers inside ourselves now that we are adults. Thus when situations come up in which we are put back into the helpless child (even though consciously we may be unaware that this is happening), we can treat ourselves abusively just to get it over with.

If only we will H.A.L.T. and feel whatever we are feeling, we will realize it is okay to feel and then lovingly respond to ourselves in our needs.

———————

Remember to H.A.L.T. today.

H.A.L.T. for incest survivors begins with *hurt.* So many of us have been numb for years because we have suffered such overwhelming and devastating hurts in our childhood. In fact, over time we came to believe that to feel at all meant to hurt.

When we begin opening to our feelings in the healing process, our hurt can seem unending.

We might not want to feel our hurt today because it can be such a powerful reminder of our betrayal and unhealed hurts of the past. But hurt is an emotional and bodily reality for all people from time to time. It is we who choose whether to feel our hurt, process the feeling and let it go or to hang onto our hurt by numbing it and putting it into cold storage with other hurts of our past. H.A.L.T. reminds us to stop our compulsive running, feel our feelings and let them go.

I am not alone in my hurts.

For most of our lives, we incest survivors have known ourselves as "never angry" but always unexpectedly "flying off the handle."

People get angry. We get angry. We need to stop and allow ourselves to feel our anger if it indeed is coming over us. There is no longer a perpetrator to abuse us for feeling this strong emotion. And no one's disapproval of our anger is an adequate reason for our denying ourselves what we really feel.

Anger can lead to violence — yes — but it need not. If we realize we are feeling angry, we can decide how to address the angering situation without doing violence to ourselves or anyone else. We will likely have much anger (even rage) about our past that has long been buried. Now is the time to accept gently these powerful feelings and direct them in positive ways toward our recovery.

Help me use anger for empowerment and freedom rather than destruction.

Lonely is feeling isolated whether in a group or all by ourselves — even if externally we are carrying on an interesting conversation. We have learned to mask our loneliness well. But now we need to stop what we are doing if we are feeling lonely. It is perfectly okay to feel lonely from time to time. It is not okay to harm or abuse ourselves rather than face our feelings of loneliness.

As children we missed out on the chance to bond with caring adults who would have accepted us even in our loneliness. We had no one to trust, no one to help us explore our feelings of what life is all about.

Our process of healing and recovery is a lot like starting from square one. But by working through our feelings of loneliness as they arise, we will find out that we are far from being alone.

I am one with millions of hurting, healing, loving, growing incest survivors.

Many of us can remember a time when the only feeling we felt safe to express about our being battered in life was "tired," not hurt, anger or loneliness. Somehow that did not leave us as vulnerable to others.

Oh yes, we were really tired. Because we could not admit what really happened, we expended a lot of energy secretly hating ourselves and then trying to convince the outside world we were okay.

In recovery's shakier moments, we might feel tired of living, but we also realize that suicide is not an option for survivors. We might feel tired because we have gotten hooked into more care-taking or compulsive working. The work of recovery can be tiring as well as freeing. Listening to our bodily feelings reminds us to take time out for rest and play.

I deserve generous portions of rest and play, renewal and refreshment.

339

Waiting can be agonizing. Waiting puts us in a passive role of expectation — and as children we learned to expect the worst. Brought up in an abusive atmosphere, however, we have tended to wait for a loving response from people who chose to abuse and betray us instead.

So after awhile we stopped waiting and began running, on the theory that it is harder to abuse a moving target. We began to see ourselves as helpless objects of other people's lust and aggression. Soon waiting itself became the enemy because we associated it with abuse.

We need to work for our healing. But like it or not, we have to wait for it too. Healing is a gradual process which we open ourselves to receive. We cannot receive if we are always on the run. We need to stop, to wait in a safe place, to open and to receive what truly heals and satisfies.

I wait for You, Healing Spirit of Love; do not disappoint me.

Birthdays mark the beginning of life in the outside world. For some, that means outside the womb; for others, birth is described as the beginning of life outside the domination of abuse.

Sure, we may have a gut reaction of cringing and tensing at the mere mention of birthdays. Birthdays of the past can hold memories of family upheaval, substance abuse, sexual abuse, betrayal and disappointment. But birthdays commemorate beginnings, not endings.

Our birthday means our life and our choice of how we are going to live it. Maybe the adults who surrounded us in our formative years were not free enough and loving enough to celebrate our birth and our existence without control and manipulation. But we now know that our life is worth celebrating and that every day holds the promise of new birth for us.

I celebrate my existence!

Trusting ourselves is a lesson we need to relearn, since our abusers robbed us of this natural gift. We learned to distrust our senses, feelings and perceptions. The world became "enemy territory" in which we did not know who could be trusted.

The healing process involves a whole program of relearning and rebuilding. By meeting and sharing with other survivors, we begin to hear positive aspects about ourselves.

As we risk ourselves in relationship — with a therapist or close friend, with fellow survivors or a sponsor — we begin to believe that we might be trustworthy people after all. But that does not really make an impact on us until we begin to trust ourselves. Trusting ourselves makes life real and enables us to open to safe places wherever we are.

I trust the valuable and lovable person who I am.

How many of us think of ourselves as innocent? Instead we tend to see ourselves as persons who have been robbed of innocence, often left feeling guilty in the process.

It is not necessarily true that people who act guilty, edgy, uneasy are exposing their true guilt. In fact, it is often the opposite with incest. The perpetrator acts as though nothing is wrong while the victim is loaded down with guilt and shame.

Not only are we innocent regarding the crime of incest, in many ways we are innocent about life. We are innocent of loving, spontaneous relationships. We are innocent with respect to healthy living. The steps, the tools and our group provide a safe place and healthy process in which to nurture our innocence to maturity.

I am innocent.

Embarking upon the healing process means opening to a degree of uncertainty about our lives. Beforehand, we made our plans and steeled ourselves against the next potential moment of abuse. But assuming a new life stance, we are often left with the question, "Now what?"

The answer that comes, disappointing as it may be, is that recovery is a process. In a dangerous world where abuse awaited us at every turn, we felt we had to know the future completely, to have it all under control, just to feel safe. But safety resides within us now and in our healing relationships. And it is through these avenues that we are in touch with our Higher Power, discerning what is next on our life's journey — and doing so one day at a time.

I am ready to take the next step.

Incest recovery is not about blame. It is about healing. That is why such remarks as "Don't drag up the past" and "Forgive and forget" are not very helpful. They are based on a fear of violence which supports denial.

But the truth is that the violence has already taken place, no matter how much people close their eyes to it. Talking about the past is a means of letting go of the violence that continues to hurt us.

It is normal to go through a stage of blaming: "You ruined my life!" Too many of us have focused the blame on ourselves. We need to separate from self-blame. Once we have sufficiently worked through our feelings about being betrayed — including anger, resentment, hatred — we can let go of blame and take hold of life.

Blaming gives away my power.

Kindness heals in a way blame cannot.

Kindness does not mean that we avoid those strong, confrontational, so-called negative feelings. It just helps us to put them into perspective. For instance, kindness during a time when we need to rage means expressing our rage without doing violence to ourself or another. It means remembering to eat when we are depressed and do not feel like eating (or not to binge on food, for those of us who handle depression in this manner).

Kindness is a new way of life in our ongoing recovery. It is learning to take care of our own needs first, rather than caretaking others. Kindness increases our ability to respond in love because we are more responsible for our own well-being. Kindness is a way of life that contradicts all the lies of abuse.

Kindness to myself is renewing my life.

Miracles and abuse appear to be at two oppo-site ends of the spectrum. In fact, as adults who have survived childhood molestation and rape, we might be inclined to call abuse reality, and miracles fantasy. After all, we hoped against hope that we would be rescued as children from the torment of abuse but, most often, no relief came.

We might have longed for human compassion and, failing to receive that, a magic rescue. That did not happen either. What we have available to us now for healing is the miracle of recovery. It is not magic by any means. Instead, it involves hard work, risk and trust. Perhaps that is why it is called miraculous.

It is a miracle, a wonder, that we were even able to survive as we did. We can accomplish so much more. Hang in there. Keep coming back.

Don't quit before your miracles.

We have all longed for the childhood we never had, a life without abuse, love without betrayal. Despite our longings, what we have so deeply hoped for has always seemed unattainable.

Our longings are inborn and only heightened by the devastation of abuse. What is it we long for? Not anything that a mere substance or activity or a fantasy family could provide. Whether we call the object (and source) of our longing God, our true self or the meaning of life, healing from incest helps put us back on track toward our goal.

But our longings have always been a part of us. We just did not know how to get them fulfilled. By following the 12 Steps of recovery one day at a time, we are shown the way.

I long for You, O God.

For many years we felt as though we had to face the struggles of life alone, unsupported. Those of us who believed in God as children either came to the conclusion that God had betrayed us by not rescuing us from the abuse or that we were completely unworthy of any divine or human love; all we deserved was abuse.

Life becomes a struggle because life in isolation is a contradiction in terms. Life means relationship, but we were often too fearful and distrusting to risk ourselves in relationship.

In our 12-Step healing process, we have come to believe that there is unconditional love for us, that there can be a deeper meaning to our lives, that we are not alone after all. Those who believe in God have finally found a healthy faith that works. Those who trust in a Higher Power by a different name also have come to believe in a source of love and life other than ourselves.

I am coming to believe there is a Higher Power who loves me just because I am.

We sexual abuse survivors revolt at any insinuation that we are insane because that touches old tapes. Abusers and co-abusers told us we were crazy when we tried to tell them what happened to us.

The truth is we were not insane when we tried to tell others. The insanity (unsoundness, unhealthiness) set in when we lived our lives accepting our abusers' lies. It is insane to go through life believing we are worthless and unlovable because another person chose to abuse us as children.

Many of us survived our traumatic childhoods by taking responsibility for our abusers' actions. It is now self-destructive. That is the insanity which we desire to become aware of and let go.

Higher Power, help me to let go of the insanity of self-hatred and embrace the sanity of self-love.

Graceful may not be the first word we associate with ourselves as survivors — but how often it is true of us! At survivor gatherings, women and men who have always felt bodily constricted and self-conscious have, in this safe atmosphere, revealed budding, graceful dancers hidden inside. And not only dancers, but artists, writers and more.

"Worthless" or "hateful" were inappropriate self-descriptions we took on from our abusers. But indeed, we are gifted, grace-filled persons.

This does not mean that we will stop hating ourselves in an instant or that we will suddenly thaw our frozen-stiff body and become ballet dancers. Accepting that we are graceful is saying a continuous "yes" to our worth and beauty.

I am graceful.

The clothes we wear are often signs of our desire to keep a safe distance from a threatening world. While some survivors emphasize style and sexuality in clothing, many of us go in for the "asexual look" in the hope that no one will notice that we are both sexual and human beings.

To hide our sexuality, however, is to try to deny the fact that we *are* female or male. As we begin to heal we will realize that it is not only okay to look good, it can be desirable as well. Being pretty, handsome, attractive, beautiful is not an open invitation to abuse. The way we dress comes to express more and more our growing self-love and self-confidence. We are strong and beautiful; we do not need to hide.

I deserve to look good.

In stores, "damaged goods" may be labeled as such and sold at clearance prices, be sent back to the factory, scrapped or given away to charity. What happens, though, to persons who are labeled "damaged goods"? More to the point, what happens to sexual abuse survivors who go through life believing we *are* damaged goods?

We see ourselves as worthless. We believe that everyone else does too — or soon will when they find out. We fail to see that our original beauty and the power of the life force within us was not erased by the violence done to us.

Indeed, our goodness, value and beauty may have gone underground after the abuse, but it has always been there. And recovery is our coming-out party.

Heal the damage so that I may experience the goodness that is my deeper reality.

We have no responsibility to any person who initiated sexual or emotional abuse against us. This is important for us to remember at any time of year, but especially during the holiday season when there is cultural pressure to put on a happy face, no matter what.

There would be no abuse without initiators. Initiators are completely responsible for the abuse. Sadly, it is rare to find an initiator who will accept responsibility and seek to make amends for the crime of incest.

As sexual abuse survivors, we are primarily responsible for our own recovery and well-being. We are not responsible for initiators — neither for protecting them nor for helping them change. Initiators will have to find their own healing path.

Higher Power, show me the way to initiate healing and a new life.

Caring for others is a sign of love which begins with the bearer of the gift. In other words, caring is not caretaking. It flows from the experience of having received unconditional love ourselves.

We experience this love through our Higher Power. Whether it comes as the inner voice of support and guidance or as the outer expression of our recovery group's concern, we begin to accept caring in a personal way.

Caring comes from the heart, grows in the heart, flows through the heart. It can be scary to open to true caring because our hearts have been wounded and abused. Yet there is no more deeply healing experience than heartfelt caring.

I care to open my heart.

There is no getting away from it. The number one time for depression is the holiday season. And why not? Merchants make millions of dollars selling empty promises of happiness. Greeting cards, television movies and social expectations portray this time of year as one of joy and family closeness.

Where is that close family? "Not here. But everyone else must have it, so let's pretend." It can be so tempting to deny the abuse once more and cover it with holiday glitter. But all the presents, sumptuous meals, decorations and alcohol cannot cover the emptiness and hurt of a family in which sexual and emotional abuse has been perpetrated, then denied. Letting go of the fantasy "greeting card" family is our first step to new life — and something to celebrate.

My present sadness is my first step toward happiness.

Enjoyment is different from partying, different from smiles and laughter, different from fun and games. Those are externals.

For years we put on the mask of the fantasy family, but that could not take away the truth of the abusive family. We may have smiled and laughed while crying and raging on the inside (all too often against ourselves). We longed for joy but found only emptiness and pain.

As we work our way through the depth of our anger, sorrow and depression, we begin to find we are making room for joy. We do not cover our other feelings with joy — that would be fake. But we make room in the garden of our hearts for joy to sprout, grow and blossom. Thus, enjoyment of life, of ourselves, becomes rooted and real for incest survivors.

The more I am coming to enjoy myself, the more I realize how much You enjoy me!

Pure . . . white . . . soft . . . steady . . . the snow falls. Browns and faded greens become brightened by its whiteness and glisten in the reflecting light. Normally fast-paced persons begin to slow — either transfixed by its beauty or cautious of the slipperiness it brings to outdoor travel.

"Pure as the driven snow" rings an almost biting phrase to the tainted-feeling survivor. How often we feel like the muddied snow — trampled, driven over and plowed to the side of the road. But just as the sun warms the once-frozen snow so that water particles rise to renewal while the grit stays behind, so does the warmth of our healing separate our inner purity from the taint of abuse. We are reminded of our inner uniqueness and purity that no sand or salt or grit of abuse can ever take away.

I am pure.

"Stinkin' thinkin' " is a phrase familiar to those who have been around AA. It applies to incest survivors too. What it refers to is a negative outlook on self, others and life that leads us to various forms of self-destructive behavior.

We tend to live as we think. If we constantly think of ourselves as damaged goods and inferior persons, how can we hope to act otherwise? But if we visualize ourselves as becoming healed and whole, day by day, we begin to live and believe that this is our true destiny.

We can influence the world through our creative energies by visualizing a world in which unconditional love is a priority, where children are loved and respected, and in which we are valued. What we visualize is truly possible, especially if we remember: "Let it begin with me."

Visualize the possibilities for love, for healing, for peace.

We who have spent years trying to uphold images of family, love and togetherness are now learning how to provide what is truly nurturing for ourselves. The choices as to how to spend our holidays are almost limitless. Solitary hiking, family gatherings or survivor meetings are some options that can be ideal holiday pastimes or disastrous undertakings, depending on our individual needs and perspectives.

Some of us find holidays too threatening and would just as soon spend them as working days so they will pass. Others have always cherished them and still do. Choosing to celebrate can be a way of saying, "This holiday has always been special to me and I refuse to let unpleasant memories of my abuser take that away from me." "Happy Holiday!" is a greeting, a wish, a blessing.

May I experience serenity throughout the holiday season.

Stilling the mind . . . opening the heart . . . Simply put, this is what meditation is about. But the goal of meditation, as understood in the 11th Step, is to improve conscious contact with the God of our understanding.

Stilling the chattering mind with its incessant inner dialogue allows us to experience silence — and possibly to hear another voice than the one in our head that is always talking. Loosening our heart from its "clenched fist" position allows for a flow of energy other than that which is always on the defensive. We become receptive.

We may choose to meditate at a certain time, in a certain posture. Or we might just find ourselves transfixed by the beauty of a sunset. It is the quiet and the openness that provides the link of a growing conscious contact with our Higher Power.

In quiet stillness I open to the Source of my being.

Good news! For everyone who has lived through victimization of sexual abuse — there is hope of healing. Good news! For those who have been frustrated with recurring flashbacks and uncontrollable tears — life gets better. Good news! For each survivor who has fought against tremendous odds just to survive the trauma of abuse — you are not alone.

There is also the good news that more and more of us are "coming out" with our abused past, thereby confronting a society that has silently tolerated such crimes. Disclosing our abuse — even to one other person — is a work of advocacy for all children and the defenseless. The good news is that we are saying no to a life of lies, betrayal and dominance, and yes to a world of acceptance, respect and nurturing love.

Good news! There is hope!

Despair is a reality for everyone victimized by incest. What can be more devastating than the trauma, betrayal, loss of having had a loved one — especially a parent — violate the most sacred trust of all, the respect for the life of one's own child?

Ironically, it is through some periods of despair that many of us have found a healing way of life. By despairing of ever living a happy life on our own, we have had the courage to reach out and find other survivors who care. Total despair can lead to death, but it need not. When we feel despairing, it may be likely that the way we have been living offers no hope. Those who have come into 12-Step fellowship, however, know that there is yet a way of hope for those who want it. Pick up the telephone. Come to a meeting. We care.

I am no longer alone.

Emptiness can be a difficult feeling to stay with. Take away the alcohol, excess food, narcotics, caretaking relationships, compulsive gambling, working or spending. Take away the fantasy family and a lifetime of pretending. Take away the hurt, anger and resentment. We are left with our "self," which can seem very empty.

By getting in touch with our emptiness through meditation, we learn to listen for inner guidance. By letting go of addictive substances, activities and relationships, we open to an emptiness which will seek the food that truly satisfies. By emptying ourselves of all that was handed to us through abuse, we touch an inner emptiness which can initially be scary but will ultimately lead to continued healing and hope.

Empty me of abuse so that I might be filled with love.

There are two kinds of fullness. The one we are very familiar with comes through overindulgence in food, drink, relationships or activities. In this type of fullness, the most we accomplish is preventing ourselves from feeling our inner emptiness for the moment. As a result we can feel "bloated" or "numb," but not really satisfied.

Satisfaction comes from the second kind of fullness, the one we are finding through our healing program of recovery from abuse.

At last we have the possibility of being filled at times with joy and gladness. At other times, pain and emptiness itself might fill us. But we realize it is okay for this to happen. This too shall pass. Then, too, we are not excluding any part of life but breathing it in to fullness and exhaling each breath in a letting go.

Fill me with life's breath.

For us incest survivors who are 20 or 80 or anywhere in-between, coming to an awareness of abuse and its effects on our lives really can be devastating. It seems as though one morning we wake up and say, "Has my whole life been wasted up to this point?" We might want to start rushing to make up for "lost time."

One perspective is to bemoan the fact that abuse and its consequences has robbed from us years of healthy living. Another view is to recognize that with recovery we have opened the door to more honest, open, healthy living.

Where should we be? How soon? A sound spiritual axiom has it that wherever we are right now is a good place to be — as long as we do not cling to it but remain open to growth. We have today, and it is our own choice as to how we will live it.

Where I am in my process right now is a good place to be.

For information on 12-Step fellowships for sexual abuse survivors contact:

Survivors of Incest Anonymous
World Service Office
P.O. Box 21817
Baltimore, MD 21222-6817

Incest Survivors Anonymous
World Service Office
P.O. Box 5613
Long Beach, CA 90805-0613